Chen Pu

Economic Reform and the Transition from Plan to Market

A Model for the Gradual Approach of Transition in China

Empirische Wirtschaftsforschung und Ökonometrie

herausgegeben von
Prof. Dr. Joachim Frohn
Universität Bielefeld

Band 1

LIT

Chen Pu

Economic Reform and the Transition from Plan to Market

A Model for the Gradual Approach of Transition in China

LIT

Die Deutsche Bibliothek – CIP-Einheitsaufnahme

Pu, Chen
Economic Reform and the Transition from Plan to Market : A Model for the Gradual Approach of Transition in China / Chen Pu . – Münster : LIT, 1996
  (Empirische Wirtschaftsforschung und Ökonometrie ; 1.)
  Zugl.: Bielefeld, Univ., Diss., 1996
  ISBN 3-8258-2908-1

NE: GT

© LIT VERLAG
  Dieckstr. 73   48145 Münster   Tel. 0251–23 50 91   Fax 0251–23 19 72

Acknowledgement

This thesis was accepted as doctoral dissertation at the faculty for economics of the University of Bielefeld.

I am especially grateful to my academic teacher, Prof. Dr. Joachim Frohn, who has introduces me to this topic and promoted the completion of this thesis by providing constructive and challenging suggestions. I would also like to thank Prof. Dr. Flaschel for his critical comments and suggestions about related literature, which had stimulating effects on the formation of this thesis in its final shape. Last but not least, I would like to thank my wife Baozhen for all her patient support.

Pu Chen

Contents

Introduction   1

Chapter 1   The Economic Reform in China   7
- 1.1   Rural Reform   7
- 1.2   Industrialization   9
- 1.3   Urban Reform   12
- 1.4   Price Reform   15
- 1.5   Shift from Plan to Market   16
- 1.6   Summary   19

Chapter 2   Basic Feature of an Economy in the Transition from Plan to Market   22
- 2.1   Centrally Planned Economy   22
  - 2.1.1   Producer in CPE   23
  - 2.1.2   The Planning Coordination   24
  - 2.1.3   The Growth Mechanism   25
  - 2.1.4   The Disequilibrium   28
- 2.2   Market Economy   29
  - 2.2.1   The Market Coordination   29
  - 2.2.2   The Growth mechanism   30
- 2.3   Economy in Transition from Plan to Market   31

Chapter 3   A Theoretical Model for Transition Process   33
- 3.1   General Approach   33
- 3.2   The Planned Economic Segment   35
- 3.3   The Market Economic Segment   38
- 3.4   Market Balance   42
- 3.5   Special Features of the Model   43
- 3.6   Equilibrium   47

Chapter 4   Existence and Uniqueness of the Equilibrium and Dynamics of the System   48
- 4.1.   Restatement of the Model   48
- 4.2   Existence and Uniqueness   50
- 4.3   Stability of the Equilibrium   53
- 4.4   Long Run Dynamics   58

Chapter 5   Analysis of the Driving Forces of the Transition   65
- 5.1   The Planned Segment and Kalecki's Model   65
- 5.2   The Market Segment and the Dualistic Economic Model   67
- 5.3   The Rural Reform and the Stimulation of Transition   68

5.4	Savings and Financial Market		71
5.5	Tax Policy		74
5.6	Adjustment of the Planned Segment		78
	5.6.1 Partial Price Adjustment		78
	5.6.2 The Dual Price		79
	5.6.3 Freeing up of the Price Control		83
5.7	Advantages in the Market Segment		85
5.8	Industrialization and Labour Distribution		87
5.9	Reform of the Labour Marekt		89
5.10	Welfare Effect of Transition		94
5.11.	Timing of the Reform		96
5.12	Feasible Transition Path		97
Chapter 6	**Numerical Studies and Empirical Relevance**		**100**
6.1.	Choice of Parameters and Initial Values		100
	6.1.1 Determination of Parameters		101
	6.1.2 The Simulation Model		105
6.2	Comparative Static with Numerical Simulations		107
	6.2.1 The Basic Transition Path		107
	6.2.2 Influence of Population Growth		110
	6.2.3 Influence of Technical Progress on the Transition		110
	6.2.4 Savings and the Distribution		113
	6.2.5 Adjustment in the Planned Segment		115
6.3.	Empirical Relevance		118

Concluding Remarks   **125**

Reference   **128**

Introduction

Since the late 1980s the market economy has been generally accepted in the post socialist countries as the only feasible economic system that could lead their economies out of crisis. In these countries the implementation of a sound functioning market economy has become the main task of the policy maker. Transition is becoming a key word in the circle of politicians and economists who are involved in the process of transition from a planned to a market economy. Although they seem to be quite optimistic about a promising future after the transition, they are continually faced with the difficulties of the actual transition process, in which the reality is less than promising for any optimism.

The main difficulty in the transformation from a planned economy to a market economy is to manage this process without big social disturbance. Generally there are two approaches to implement the transition. The first one is known as the „big bang" approach, which tries to establish a totally new market based framework, by radical breaking down the old planned economic institution. At the outset, the planned economy – the state-owned enterprises and the planning commissions with all the functions of coordination and distribution – is the dominant, if not sole, part of the whole economy. If this planned economy were to be rendered disfunctional through a shock, it would not only require a huge financial investment but also lead to massive social problems, such as a fall in domestic production, unemployment, and shortage of supply. The present transition crisis[1] in the post-socialist countries of eastern Europe exemplifies the consequences of the „big bang"-policy. The second approach, known as the gradual approach, is a pragmatic policy of transition –„step by step". This kind of policy does not put the elimination of the planned economy in the forefront. On the contrary, it tries to introduce market activities into the economy and promotes them, while keeping the planned economy functioning as before and reforming it step by step. The economic reform in China followed typically the gradual approach. During the economic reform, the Chinese GNP recorded one of the fastest growths in the world, and China seems to be well on its way from plan to market.

This thesis considers the questions related with the gradual approach to economic transition using the Chinese economy as an empirical background. To introduce market activities into the economy dominated by the planned economic activities is to establish an economical and legal framework for enterprises which operate according to the market principle, while keeping the planned economy functioning. In this context there emerge questions, such as: is it possible for the two different

---

[1] Schmieding, Holger (1993): 'From Plan to Market: On the Nature of Transition Crisis'; Weltwirtschaftliches Archiv Vol.129(2) 1993; p.217-218.

economic activities to co-exist side by side in a common economic environment? How will they act on each other with respect to the production, the distribution of the income, and the growth of the production; How will the relative weight of each kind of activity affect the whole economy? Which type of economic activities will dominate in the long run? To describe the transition process and to answer the questions above is the main concern in this thesis.

Of course, an institutional framework has to be set up for the market activities to function. This institutional framework is in itself an important issue in the transition from the planned to the market economy. It has become the most discussed topic in literature about the transition. Perkins, for instance, listed 5 conditions for the reform to be successful.[2] Byrd discussed the prerequisites for an effectively functioning market.[3] In this thesis we will take the existence of the necessary conditions for market activities as given, without discussing them. The main concern here is what will happen if the market comes into being.

The thesis consists of six chapters. In the first chapter we will give a short review of the economic reform in China, based on which the theoretical model is constructed. In particular, we will discuss those reform measures that promote the transition from plan to market. The rural reform was one of the most important elements of the economic reform. It changed the economic structure and raised the production in the agriculture, improved the income of farmers, promoted the capital accumulation in rural areas, and hence stimulated a decentralised industrialisation process. The newly emerged industrial enterprises became the most important component of the market segment. Furthermore we will examine the industrialisation process and its role in the transition from plan to market. The urban reform with the „two-tiers"-system at its centre legitimated the existence of the market segment. The „two-tiers"-system separated industrial production and the supply of industrial products into two parts, in which one part was integrated into the centrally planned system and the other part coordinated through the market mechanism. The „two-tiers"-system has favoured relative advantages of the market segment and has promoted the growth in the market segment. With the rapid growth of the market segment, a shift from plan to market took place. Hence, the Chinese transition from plan to market is called „growing out of the plan". At the end of this chapter, we will summarise the particularity of the transition in China in four hypotheses, which compose the main ideas used in the construction of the theoretical model.

---

[2] Perkins, Dwight (1994): „Completing Chinese Reform", Journal of Economic Perspective, spring 1994, p.27 ff.
[3] For details see Byrd, William A. (1991), pp.19 ff.

In the second chapter, we will outline the main features of the economy in the transition from plan to market. Because the economy contains both planned economic and market economic elements during the transition, at least in the gradual version of transition, we will examine the features of centrally planned economy (CPE) and the free market economy (FME) respectively. In order to characterise the centrally planned economy, we will restate some of the theoretical and empirical contributions in this field. Kornai's theory on the economics of shortage and the growth theory developed by Kalecki for the socialist economy are the main theoretical sources used in the description of the CPE. We will use the classical theory on the market economy to describe market activities. In the forefront of the description is the macro behaviour and the growth mechanism of each system. At the end of this chapter we will classify the possible transition forms, according to the difference of their natures, into two groups - the intrinsic transition and the extrinsic transition.

On the basis of the description in chapter 2, a two-segment-model is constructed, where the economy is divided according to the institutional conditions of the activities into a planned economic segment and a market economic segment. The „planned economic segment" and the „market economic segment" are to be understood as an institutional setting with the functions of resource allocation, coordination of production, and distribution of the products. This formal model provides a framework to demonstrate the interaction of the two economic segments within a closed economy. The production technologies in both segments are assumed to be neo-classical. Based on the fact that during the transition the capital is always the bottleneck of the economy, we assume that the capital will be fully utilised. The labour utilisation is determined according to marginal productivity. With regard to the labour distribution, the composition of final demand and the production features, a dualistic economic structure is constructed in the model in order to take into account the significant structural difference between agriculture and industry in the Chinese economy.

Because the main interest does not lie in modelling the planning behaviour, the planned prices and the allocation of the capital stock in the planned segment are treated exogenously. Other variables of the planned segment are determined according to these prices. The character of the planned economic segment is expressed mainly through its essential features, namely the rigid price, the inflexible resource allocation, and the disequilibrium. The change of plan variables is described as the adjustments of the planning authority, which are forced through the competition of the market segment.

Without the market segment, the shortage of supply of consumer goods will result in forced savings, which are used to finance the demand for investment goods through the central planning authority. The enterprises of the market segment can take advantage of this unsatisfied demand and get an easy entrance to the market.

The producers in the market segment are assumed to be price-takers and try to maximise their profit. The market mechanism functions mainly through the flexible prices, the flexible production and the flexible allocation of resources, and keeps total demand and total supply in balance. This balance is not the equality between supply and demand within the market segment, but is the equality between supply and demand in the whole economy with the unequal prices in the two segments. This balance is understood as an equilibrium. In this sense, the model can be viewed as a general equilibrium model, with a planned segment in which prices and resource allocations are determined exogenously according to central planning, and a market segment in which the market mechanism tries to correct the distortion produced by the planned segment and keep the whole economy in equilibrium through a flexible price and efficient resource allocation.

In chapter 4 we will examine the conditions for the existence of temporal equilibrium and the growth path derived from temporal equilibria. The difference in the institutional settings of the producers results in the different economic performances of the two segments. Different factor pricing, distinct combinations of factors, and different income distributions lead to unequal growth rates in both segments. The difference in the growth rates, in this case the more accelerated growth of the market segment, is considered the engine of the transition from plan to market. Because of the difference in the growth rates, the share of each segment in the whole economy will change. The path of the expanding share of the market segment and the shrinking share of the planned segment may be viewed as explicit description of the transition from plan to market.

In chapter 5 we will examine factors that may influence the transition process. We will begin with factors that may affect the extrinsic transition i.e. the different growth mechanisms in the two segments, the saving behaviour, and the distribution of savings for investment in the two segments. Then we will examine the factors that determine the intrinsic transition. Facing the faster growth in the market segment and the shrinking share of the planned segment, the executives in the planned segment try in various ways to adjust to the new situation. We will study the impact of different adjustment policies in the planned economic segment. We will discuss the most important issues in the economic reform – the price reform, the financial market reform, and the labour market reform. Following a discussion of the reform policies, the importance of correct timing of a policy will be considered. We will also examine the welfare gains of different participants in the economy during the transition process. At the end of this chapter we will present a feasible transition path and try to resolve the question, whether the planned and market segments can co-exist in the long run.

Chapter 6 involves some numerical simulations of the model. From the discussion in chapter 4 and chapter 5, we will have gained an understanding of the qualitative properties of the model. We try to demonstrate these properties in chapter 6 through numerical simulations. We will also show the alternative transitional paths due to different policies and various economic conditions. Finally, we will simulate the realised development and compare the numerical simulation with the empirical observations in order to provide a theoretical explanation.

In the last chapter, the main conclusions of this study will be summarised.

Chapter 1

The Economic Reform in China

1.1 Rural Reform

The Chinese economic reform began with the agricultural reform, which was officially announced in the third Congress of the 11th Plenum of the Communist Party in December 1978. The reform aimed at the reorganisation of the production structure in the rural area in order to achieve better performance in the agricultural production. In the 1950s, the Chinese agriculture had experienced great success. In 1957 the total agricultural production surpassed all previous records. During the late 1960s and the 1970s, great effort was made to improve the performance of the collective production[4]. There were campaigns lasting decades to promote the development of agricultural production all over the country. In spite of this, agricultural production showed stagnation from the 1960s to the end of the 1970s. Still worse, in 1976 and 1977 the per capita grain production fell slightly back due to the rapid growth of the population.

Table 1.1 Agricultural production

(1) Year	(2) Grain (Mio.T)	(3) Population (Mio.)	(2)/(3)
1952	16392	57482	0,28
1957	19505	64653	0,30
1962	16000	67295	0,23
1965	19453	72538	0,26
1970	23996	82992	0,28
1975	28452	92420	0,30
1976	28631	93717	0,30
1977	28737	94974	0,30
1978	30477	96259	0,31
1979	33212	97542	0,34
1980	32056	98705	0,32
1981	32502	100072	0,32
1982	35450	101654	0,34

---

[4]In the campaign known as 'Learn from Dazai' that was set as a model of collective production by Mao Zedong, every production team was called to cultivate a standerd field called the Dazai-field and to adapt the experience of Dazai in the organisation of production.

1983	38728	103008	0,37
1984	40731	104357	0,39
1985	37911	105851	0,35
1986	39151	107507	0,36
1987	40298	109300	0,36
1988	39408	111026	0,35
1989	40755	112704	0,36
1990	44624	114333	0,39
1991	43529	115823	0,37
1992	44266	117171	0,37
1993	45648	118517	0,38
1994	44510	119850	0,37

Source: Chinese Statistic Year Book 1993 p.248, p.97
Chinese Statistic Year Book 1995 p.247

This was the very reason that a reform in agriculture was undertaken. Moreover, the Chinese leadership had learned from the lessons made during the campaign of „great leap forwards" in the late 50s, namely that there would be no growth in the whole economy if there is no growth in the agriculture[5]. Due to the impatience of realising „the four modernisations"[6], the rural reform became a political task of first rank.[7]

The experience of the early 60s naturally served as a reference for the rural reform. At the beginning, the reform was just the come-back of Liu and Deng's economic consolidation policy in the early 1960s, which had successfully led China out of the economic crisis at the end of 1950s[8].

---

[5] The following was written in the Kommunique of the third Congress of the 11th Plenum of Communist Party China, „Die rasche Entwicklung der gesamten Wirtschaft und die ununterbrochene Hebung des Lebensstandards des ganzen Volks basieren darauf, daß die Landwirtschaft energisch wiederhergestellt und beschleunigt entwickelt wird." Peking Rundschau 1978,
Vol. 52 p.13

[6] The four modernizations were: modernization of agriculture, modernization of industry, modernization of notional defence, and modernization of science and technology. The four modernizations had been set as the main political target by the communist party of China in the middle 1970s.

[7] Fan Gang explained the starting of reform in agricultur in a 'least resistence' approach. Fan Gang (1994), p.99 ff.

[8] After the failure of Mao's „great leap forewords", Chinese economy fell into a serious crisis. In the line of the consolidation policy of Liu Shaoqi and Deng Xiaopin, markets of agricultural products and sideline products were given free and the collective communes were reorganised in family-based production. With the consolidation policy the economy recovered very soon. This

The so called „household responsibility system" and the freeing up of the market for agriculture products and sideline products constituted the principle components of the rural reform, supported by an increase of planned purchasing prices for agricultural products. The key words for this reform were „incentive" and „efficiency".

The „household responsibility system" transformed the collective production teams, which consisted of about 10 to 100 families, into household-based production organisation. The households were offered the right to use the farmland for 10 to 20 years and were promised a prolongation. As repayment the household was obligated to sell a certain amount of their crops to the state at the planned price. Beyond this, the household could decide on production independently and could dispose the rest of the production and the profit freely. Within two years, the decollectivization was almost completed. At the end of 1980, the government announced that there was to be no more direct intervention in the production plan of the farmers[9].

The freeing up of the market for agricultural products and sideline products was carried out through the promotion of activities in the existing markets and fairs. Instead of the strict control as practised before the reform, various infrastructures were provided for the markets and fairs. The markets and fairs in the rural area had always been one of the most important opportunities for the farmers to get their money income. Although they had already existed before the rural reform, they were tightly controlled by the local government. The control was carried out more through ideological pressure rather than through a strict price administration. Even before the reform, prices on the markets and fairs were negotiated. In short, the existing markets and fairs served as a good starting point for the development of market economic activities[10].

The „household responsibility system" and the favourable market situation, which was strongly supported by an expanded demand due to the increase of wages in the industrial sector and an increase in planned price for agricultural products, generated a great incentive for the farmers to raise their production. The success of the rural reform responded very soon.

---

policy ceased, however, with the beginning of the culture revolution and had been criticised as 'revisionism'.
[9] See Peking Rundschau Vol.50 1980, p.4.
[10] For details about the existing market, compare Byrd, William (1991), p.44 ff.

Table 1.2 Agricultural development during the rural reform

Year	Index of net production value	Index of labour productivity in agriculture	Annual income per Capita (Yuan)	Labourers employed in agriculture (Mio.)
1978	161,1	0,57	133,57	284
1979	171,5	0,60	-	287
1980	168,4	0,58	191,33	292
1981	180,4	0,60	-	298
1982	201,6	0,65	-	309
1983	218,7	0,70	309,77	312
1984	247	0,80	355,33	309
1985	253,7	0,81	379,6	312
1986	261,4	0,83	423,76	313
1987	273,2	0,86	462,55	317
1988	279,4	0,86		323
1989	288,3	0,87		333
1990	309,9	0,91	686,31	342
1991	317	0,91	708.55	350
1992	332,9	0,96	783,99	349
1993	344,7	1,01	921,62	339
1994	358,6	1,07	1220,98	333

Source: Chinese Statistic Year Book 1995 p.32, p.83 and p.279
Chinese Statistic Year Book 1993 p.98, p.34, and p.277
Chinese Statistic Year Book 1988 p. 823

From 1978 to 1984 the growth of grain production was very remarkable (see **Table 1.1**). During the first 7 years of the reform, the growth rate of productivity was 6.09%. This kind of improvement in grain production seemed to be exhausted until 1984. After 1984 the grain production seemed to have reached the point of saturation. However, production in agriculture got a further development through sideline production. The index of net production value grew continuously (see **Table 1.2**). It was not only an extensive growth, which is typical in a soviet-style economy, but also a growth of productivity due to better organisation and better management in agriculture.

1.2 Industrialisation

Based on an improved financial situation in the rural area, the so called township-village enterprises (TVEs) were founded in large numbers. They are mostly engaged in non-agricultural production. The rural area underwent an industrialisation process during the reform period. This development can be clearly seen in the composition of the social products in the rural area (see **Table 1.3**).

Table 1.3 The composition of the total social products in the rural area

Year	Total (100Mio.)	Agr. (100Mio.)	Ind. (100Mio.)	Constr. (100Mio.)	Transp. (100Mio.)	Trade (100Mio.)
1980	2792,12	1922,6	543,96	179,97	47,14	98,45
1983	4123,78	2750	826,49	320,88	82,63	143,78
1984	5067,55	3214,13	1161,31	370,58	132,55	188,98
1985	6340,04	3619,49	1750,08	510,49	190,42	269,56
1986	7554,23	4013,01	2380,79	591,93	245,4	323,1
1987	9431,61	4675,7	3284,86	723,31	334,47	413,27
1988	12534,69	5865,27	4781,16	895,33	434,44	558,49
1989	14480,17	6534,73	5886,02	919,17	515,5	624,75
1990	16619,21	7662,09	6719,13	978,47	579,62	679,3
1991	19004,09	8057,03	8266,5	1142,32	660,76	777,48
1992	25386,28	9084,71	12717,09	1570,01	906,04	1108,43

Share of each Sectors					
Year	Agr.	Ind.	Constr.	Transp	Trade
1980	68,86	19,48	6,45	1,69	3,53
1983	66,69	20,04	7,78	2,00	3,49
1984	63,43	22,92	7,31	2,62	3,73
1985	57,09	27,60	8,05	3,00	4,25
1986	53,12	31,52	7,84	3,25	4,28
1987	49,57	34,83	7,67	3,55	4,38
1988	46,79	38,14	7,14	3,47	4,46
1989	45,13	40,65	6,35	3,56	4,31
1990	46,10	40,43	5,89	3,49	4,09
1991	42,40	43,50	6,01	3,48	4,09
1992	35,79	50,09	6,18	3,57	4,37

Source: Chinese Statistic Year Book 1993, p.333

During the first 7 years of the rural reform, production was still concentrated in agriculture, whereas after 1985 it was shifting continuously from agricultural to industrial production.

By the end of 1991, industrial production outweighed the agricultural production in the rural area. Obviously, the economic reform was marked by a rapid development from rural-agricultural to urban-industrial activities in terms of dualistic economics. The TVEs were founded through self-financing, and therefore independent from any state planning. From the very beginning they operated according to the market principle, because their existence depended fully on their economic success. Due to the increasing share of the production of the TVEs in the whole economy, market activities played a more and more important role in the economy. A shift from plan to market took place continuously with the industrialisation process. This decentralised industrialisation became a driving force for the transition from plan to market. The TVEs are now the most active force in Chinese Economy (see **Table 1.4**).[11]

Table 1.4 Gross output value of industry (100 Mio.)

Year	State-owned enterprises (1)	Township- and village enterprises (2)	Ratio (2)/(1)
1978	3289	358	0,11
1979	3673	423	0,12
1980	3915	509	0,13
1981	4037	579	0,14
1982	4326	646	0,15
1983	4739	757	0,16
1984	5262	1245	0,24
1985	6302	1827	0,29
1986	6971	2413	0,35
1987	8250	3243	0,39
1988	10351	4529	0,44
1989	12342	5244	0,42
1990	13063	6050	0,46
1991	14954	8780	0,59
1992	17824	13635	0,76
1993	22724	23446	1,03
1994	26200	32336	1,23

Source: Chinese Statistic Year Book 1993 p.396 and p.412
Chinese Statistic Year Book 1995 p.365 and p.379

---

[11] For a detailed discussion about township- village enterprises, see Shen Guanbao (1991) p.158 ff.

Although it is questionable whether the sudden changes in the figures of 1984 and 1992 are reliable, there is no doubt that the TVEs are playing an increasingly important role in the economy.

The dramatic development of the TVEs is favoured by the following factors: (1) The rural reform freed the farmers from the tight organisation of the early production teams. The increased productivity in agriculture made it possible for the peasants to engage themselves in non-agricultural production. The newly established incentive system promoted an entrepreneurial spirit, and the rapidly raised income in the rural area formed the starting capital for entrepreneurial undertakings. (2) A comprehensive market was established, consisting of markets and fairs in the rural area, and the so-called secondary market in addition to the planned economy, which was tolerated and later accepted by the planning authority during the economic reform. Within the „two-tiers"-system this secondary market was legitimated and developed rapidly. This market became the environment of independent enterprises, since both input and output were available and could be sold on the market. (3) The disequilibrium situation of the planned segment – the unsatisfied demand of state-owned enterprises and consumers – favoured the existence and growth of the TVEs[12]. (4) The support of the local governments was also very important for the growth of TVEs. Because the TVEs were the most important income source for the local governments, they supported the enterprises by providing infrastructure, and especially by gathering credit for the enterprises. (5) The widespread industrial sector, which developed during the three decades before the reform, provided sufficient technological precondition for the TVEs to start the industrialisation in the rural area. In particular, the location of industry in the underdeveloped rural areas, which was pursued during the cultural revolution as a strategic policy, revealed the long-term effect in the 80s and 90s.

Table 1.4 shows that from 1978 to 1992 the ratio of gross production value of the TVEs to that of the state-owned enterprises increased from 0.11 to 0.76. Hence, the production growth of township village enterprises accounts for a great part of the overall growth of the economy. These figures indicate the typical Chinese pattern of the transition: growing out of plan.

1.3 Urban Reform

„Incentive" and „efficiency" were also the key words in the urban reform. Similar to the start of rural reform, the first reform effort in industry was carried out around 1980 by re-executing the consolidation policy of the early 1960s. This was designed to improve the performance of the state-owned enterprises within a

---

[12] Peking Rundschau 1983 Vol.50 P.22-26.

framework dominated by mandatory output planning and administrative allocation of inputs and products through a restricted material incentive system.[13] This reform consisted mainly of two components. First, the state-owned enterprises were allowed to retain a modest share of total profits, which previously had to be completely transferred to the state, so that now the state-owned enterprises would have more incentive to perform more efficiently. The free disposal of this profit on the enterprise level expanded the activities outside the plan, even if they were very modest at the very beginning. Second, a premium system was reintroduced to the industrial enterprises to motivate both executives and workers. This was the first increment of the average wage for more than 20 years. This policy led to a growth of the final demand and created favourable conditions for the formation of free markets in the economy.

The result of these reform measures was the establishment of a material incentive and expansion of the activities outside the planned economy. The response to the reform can be seen in **Table 1.5**.

In comparison to the success of agriculture between 1978 and 1984, the achievement of industry during the same time period was very modest. This difference in development was compelling enough to adopt the experience of the rural reform for industry. Meanwhile, the secondary market had expanded massively. Many transactions were made outside the central plan[14]. The executives of the state-owned enterprises knew well the advantage of selling products on the secondary market at a higher price. Hence, a strong desire arose for a price reform from the state-owned enterprises.

Table 1.5 Growth rates in state-owned industry and in agriculture (nominal)

Year	Output of state-owned enterprises (100Mio.)	Output of agriculture (100Mio.)	Growth rate of output in agriculture	Growth rate of output in state-owned enterprises
1978	3289	1379		
1979	3673	1698	0,23	0,12
1980	3915	1923	0,13	0,07
1981	4037	2181	0,13	0,03
1982	4326	2486	0,14	0,07
1983	4739	2750	0,11	0,10
1984	5262	3214	0,17	0,11

---

[13] See also Jefferson and Rawski (1994), p.50 ff.
[14] For details see: Wu Jinglian and Zhao Renwei (1987), p.319 ff.

1985	6302	3620	0,13	0,20
1986	6971	4013	0,11	0,11
1987	8250	4676	0,17	0,18

Source: Chinese Statistic Year Book 1988 p. 37 and Chinese Statistic Year Book 1993 p. 412.

In 1984 a further set of reforms was undertaken, which consisted of the "tow-tiers system" and the "contract responsibility system". Quite in the spirit of the traditional Chinese philosophy school of the golden mean, the „two-tiers system" was neither a clear decision for market nor for plan, but merely a mixture of them. In the „two-tiers" system, the supply of industrial products was portioned into planned and market economic components. The central planning covered only a part of the production capacity. The transaction within the plan supply was made at planned prices. This planned supply was formally guaranteed through the contract responsibility system. Under this system the enterprise had to fulfil specified obligations, which normally included typically, the amount of production and profits which had to be delivered to the state. Beyond these obligations, the enterprises were encouraged to produce and sell their products on the market at the market price, which responded to relation of supply and demand on the market.

The „two-tiers" system legitimated the activities in the existing secondary market and promoted these kinds of market activities[15]. Because the activities on the market had a higher financial return than the activities within the plan, profit-oriented enterprises had no incentive for investment in the plan portion; instead they put their funds in the more profitable market portion. This led to the tendency towards „growing out of the plan". „This tendency to grow out of the plan could be offset by investment funds being ploughed into expansion of the planned sector. But the state budget now accounts for a much lower share of the total investment than in the past"[16] (see **Table 1.6**). Based on activities outside of the central planning, a large number of new profit-oriented enterprises were founded. Although many of them were supported by state-owned or collective enterprise, thus belonging, so far the property right is concerned, to the group of state-owned or collective enterprises, they were not integrated into any planning. They operated as independent enterprises, whose existence and growth depended fully on their economic success. Accordingly, a new type of employment emerged, the so called "contract worker". In contrast to the traditional employment relationship in state-owned enterprises, where employees were hired for their life with all the social

---

[15]For a detail discussion about the impact of the two tiers system on the economy ses:Byrd, William A. (1987) p.295-308
[16]Compare: Byrd, William A.(1987), p.299.

benefits, the contract workers were hired for a limited time, and generally, with only a minimum of social benefits.

In general, we can say that with the introduction of the „two-tiers system" an economic framework for market activities began to be established, though this framework was not at all clearly defined, many important questions such as property rights, ownership, legal basis of an enterprise etc. remained and have yet to be answered.

1.4 Price Reform

At the very beginning of the reform, the importance of a market-oriented price formation was already recognised by the reformers. Various reform measures were undertaken to drive the price away from bureaucratic control towards the market price formation.

In line with the rural reform, the market for agricultural sideline products was set free, and prices were flexibly determined according to the demand and the supply situation on the market. This was the first step in the price reform. Since 1984, in correspondence with the „two-tiers system", a so called „dual price system" was practised in the economy. The „dual price system" meant that there were two different prices for the same kind of products in the economy. As some of the products had to be sold at the planned price according to the plan, the others could be dealt on the market at a market price, which was, in general, much higher than the planned price.

Before the introduction of the „dual price system", the transaction outside the central plan and the flexible prices were viewed as activities in the „grey strip". The „dual price system" provided a kind of legal basis for these activities. With the introduction of the „dual price system", prices of a large category of goods were set totally free. Actually, the number of the categories of materials controlled by the state was reduced from 256 to 23 in 1985[17]. At the end of the 1980s most prices were set free except the prices for basic food, energy products, and few raw materials. In 1993 even the prices for basic foods were freed from planning.

Along with the progress in the price reform, a material incentive system was gradually forming. The market saw a flourish of development after 1984. Through involvement in market activities, the executives of the state-owned enterprises became more and more conscious of the economic interest related to the autonomy

---

[17]For details see: Wu and Zhao (1987) p.312 ff.

of enterprises. Although the „dual price system" and the „two-tiers system" were originally designed to make the economy more flexible and more efficient with the help of market elements in the planned economy, they also generated unexpected effects, which directly influenced the plan execution and forced the plan system to change itself. Wu and Zhao summarised these effects as „hypocritical behaviour by enterprises, loss of objective standard for performance assessment by the state, induced smuggling in distribution and irrational utilisation of resources"[18]. The effects pictured negatively by Wu and Zhao, only expressed that the forces of market went their own way whether it was wished or not. The plan became more and more indicative[19]. The objects of central planning shifted over from the targets of the enterprises on the micro level to economic variables on the macro level.

1.5 Shift from Plan to Market

The response to the „two-tiers system" was immediate and tremendous. The data from the National Conference on Material Flow in early 1986 indicated that the planned allocation of coal, timber, steel and cement to enterprises fell respectively by 50%, 30.7%, 56.9% and 19.4% in 1985[20]. Surveys of state-owned enterprises show a clear shift from plan to market. The share of material input purchased through the market rose from 12% to 66%, from 1980 to 1989[21]. The output sold on the market rose from 13% to 66% in the same period of time[22]. The investment financed by bank credits and by self-financing of the enterprises took a continuously larger share in the whole investment. (see **Table 1.6**)

In an increasingly market-like environment, where incentive was established, the competence of the enterprise had increased and the competition from the market was effective, the state-owned enterprises tended to become a cost minimiser. Empirical evidence confirms this tendency[23].

---

[18]Wu and Zhao (1987), p. 312 ff.
[19]For details see: Naughton, Barry (1990), p.743-767.
[20]Source: Wu and Zhao Dual (1987),p.309-318.
[21]Caimao Jinji 1992 3-15
[22]Compare: Jefferson Rawski (1994) p.51.
[23]Compare: Jefferson and Rawski (1994) p.55.

Table 1.6 Composition of investment

year	1981	1982	1983	1984	1985	1986	1987
state allocated	269,7	279,2	339,71	421	407,8	440,6	475,5
bank credit	122	176,1	175,5	258,4	510,27	638,3	835,9
self financing	532,8	714,5	848,3	1082	1533,6	1808	2154
foreign investment	36,36	60,51	66,55	70,66	91,48	132,1	175,3
total	961,0	1230	1430,0	1832	2543,1	3019	3640

Shares of the investment

state allocated	0,28	0,23	0,24	0,23	0,16	0,15	0,13
bank credit	0,13	0,14	0,12	0,14	0,20	0,21	0,23
self financing	0,55	0,58	0,59	0,59	0,60	0,60	0,59
foreign invstment	0,04	0,05	0,05	0,04	0,04	0,04	0,05

year	1988	1989	1990	1991	1992	1993	1994
state allocated	410	342	388	373	334	463	529
bank credit	927	716	871	1292	2152	2925	3703
self financing	2901	2356	2329	2879	4025	6218	8001
foreign investment	259	274	278	316	457	907	1768
total	4497	4137	4449	5509	7855	12457	16370

Shares of the investment

state allocated	0,09	0,08	0,09	0,07	0,04	0,03	0,03
bank credit	0,21	0,17	0,20	0,23	0,27	0,23	0,22
self financing	0,65	0,57	0,52	0,52	0,51	0,49	0,49
foreign investment	0,06	0,07	0,06	0,06	0,06	0,07	0,10

Source: Chinese Statistic Year Book 1988 p.559
Chinese Statistic Year Book 1993 p.145
Chinese Statistic Year Book 1995 p.137

Even more far-reaching was the impact of the „dual price system", with its built-in-dynamics to overcome the planning system altogether. The large price difference between the plan price and the market price and the increased involvement in the market resulted in a rapid rise in costs and a fall in profits in the state-owned enterprises, so that the government revenue from the enterprises could not benefit from the growth in the industry.

Table 1.7 Costs and profit of the state-owned enterprises

Year	Profit+tax (100Mio.)	Costs (100Mio.)	Growth rate of profit+tax	Growth rate of costs
1978	790,7	2208,39		
1979	846,4	2474,96	0,07	0,12
1980	907,1	2681,11	0,07	0,08
1981	923,3	2771,02	0,02	0,03
1982	972,2	3020,61	0,05	0,09
1983	1032,8	3301,54	0,06	0,09
1984	1152,8	3717,48	0,12	0,13
1985	1334,1	4585,06	0,16	0,23
1986	1341,4	5242,43	0,01	0,14
1987	1514,1	6246,95	0,13	0,19
1988	1774,9	7893,28	0,17	0,26
1989	1773,14	9682,25	0,00	0,23
1990	1503,14	10430,8	-0,15	0,08
1991	1661,15	11887,9	0,11	0,14
1992	1944,12	14804,29	0,17	0,25
1993	2454,70	17278,22	0,26	0,16
1994	2876,25	17601,06	0,17	0,018

Source: Chinese Statistic Year Book 1993 p.430
Chinese Statistic Year Book 1994 p.399
Chinese Statistic Year Book 1995 p.402

This fact inevitably produced a strong pressure from both the enterprises and from the planning authority to raise the plan price. An adaptive adjustment of the plan price to the market price took place.

The increase of the production capacity in the market segment and the adaptive adjustment of the plan price to the market price led to the convergence of the two prices. This process went so far that the plan allocation lost more and more on effectiveness. For example, in 1992 the difference between the state-controlled grain price and the market price was so negligible that most people bought their grain from a private supplier for better service. The price for grains, hence, was set totally free in 1993. In the same year the plan allocation accounted only for 7% of the total industrial production[24].

1.6 Summary

The Chinese economy has experienced one of the fastest growth periods of all countries in the world in the last 15 years. It seems to be on the way towards a successful transition from a planned to a market economy, while most other post-socialist countries suffer from economic and social problems – the so called transition crisis. The question naturally arises: what are the specific reasons for the Chinese economy to perform so differently than the economies of the post-socialist countries? To answer this question we can sketch out four hypotheses as a means to summarise the special Chinese development.

The first hypothesis is that the gradual approach to the transition from plan to market in China has protected the old economic structure and the planned economic mechanism from a sudden collapse and thus avoided a radical decline of the domestic production, with which social disturbance would always be connected. The transition is driven by the rapid growth of the newly emerged market sector in the economy. The state-owned enterprises did not suffer from any radical structure changes. On the contrary, they have profited from the general favourable economic boom situation in such a way so that they could develop rather well.

This gradual approach to the transition was, in fact, a de facto result of economic development stimulated by a series of reform policies, most of which were originally designed to enforce the growth of the planned economy and were, by no means, aimed at any kind of transition towards a market economy[25]. The built-in mechanism of market had driven the Chinese economy on the way to a market economy. In this sense, the transition in China was a „by-product" of the economic reform rather than a designed political target.

In the Communiqué of the third congress of the 11th plenum of the CPC, which is considered the document of the beginning of the economic reform, the market was not a topic. The word 'market' did not even appear in the document. Obviously, the policy makers had not given any thought to the market. The reform effort in the industry in 1979 was designed to give the state-owned enterprises more vitality and to let them work more actively by setting up a material incentive system in the state-owned enterprises, but not to make any essential change in the planned economic system.

---

[24] Source: Su in Jefferson and Rawski (1994) p.69.
[25] Perkins, Dwight (1994), p.24

In the „CCCP Decision about the Economic System Reform", which is considered as the most important document on the urban reform in 1984, it was stated that „the socialist economy is a planned commodity economy based on public ownership. It is not a market economy, which is fully regulated by market mechanism." At that time, policy makers were aware of some functions of market through the successful reform practice in the rural area, but they were not willing to give up the doctrine of the „superiority of planned economy". „The planned economy should play the central role and the market adjustment should play the subsidiary role." The policy makers wanted to make the planned economy more effective with the help of market, which had done very well in the agriculture. The „two-tiers system" and the „dual price system" were supposed to give the state-owned enterprises more autonomy, so that they could better cope with the new situation in the economy and that the economy might function more efficiently. „Plan influencing and market fine tuning" summarises the main idea of this policy.

In 1987 the second stage of urban reform began. There was no remarkable political intention in the direction of transition from plan to market. The political design of the policy makers stayed on the level of 1984. In the document of the 13th Plenum of the CCCP, the economy was defined as „ a socialist planned commodity-economic system, which should be an inherent unity of plan and market." The wide spread of the „responsibility contract system" was an experiment in seeking a new organisational form in the planned economy.

In 1992, decentralised market activities had long since been a reality in the economy. With the breaking down of the socialist block in eastern Europe, „planned economy" was naturally associated with „failure economy". To rescue itself from the political crisis which had lasted since 1989, policy makers in China urgently needed a new orientation. The „socialist market economy" as a political slogan was born in this situation. Although in the reality no one knew how this system should function, the combination of 'socialist' and 'market economy' is something, which the policy makers had been searching for. On the one hand, the attribute „socialist" claimed the leading pretension of the Communist Party of China, on the other hand, through the phrase „market economy", a difference was to be made clear between the Communist Party of China and its former colleagues in eastern Europe. The economic reform in China is still a project without a blueprint. Why, however, is there any need for a blueprint, now that it has done well without any blueprint?

The second hypothesis is that the rural reform and the urban reform changed the industrialisation mechanism in the economy and provided favourable conditions for a decentralised industrialisation and urbanisation process. This process was characterised by a rapid growth of the non-agricultural production in the rural area. The share of industrial production in the domestic production increased rapidly. As the result of decentralised industrialisation, the newly formed TVEs and other non-state-owned enterprises were profit-oriented. These profit-oriented enterprises took the advantage of their flexibility and could grow faster then the state-owned enterprises. Consequently, the share of planned activities in the economy decreased, while the share of market activities increased. In short, the rapid growth led to a special pattern of transition -„growing out of plan".

The third hypothesis is that rapid market oriented growth has widely hidden the structural problems[26], which are inevitable in the reform of the old economic structure with the planned economic organisation and the planned co-ordination system. On the one hand, rapid growth of the market activities could have overweighed the decline of production, which would have occurred if there had not been such a rapid growth of market activities. On the other hand, rapid growth of market activities enhanced the market force and strengthened competition in the economy. This, in turn, motivated and forced policy-makers to adjust planned activities to the new situation and make the planned segment become more and more market-like as this seemed to be the only way for it to survive in the economy.

To interpret the reform measures as a forced adjustment to the market situation sheds new light on the gradual approach of reform. We could compare the Chinese policy-maker without a blueprint with a „blind" man, who could not see the way from plan to market, but the challenge from the market segment served him as a best „seeing-eye dog", who instinctively knew the way to market.

The fourth hypothesis is the logical implication of the former three. If the former three hypotheses are correct, the issues about the transition from plan to market will be passé, since the existing market force will drive the transition process automatically. The policy makers do not need to bother any more about how to promote the transition process. The main focus of the attention should be how to cope with the negative effects of the market economy.

---

[26]For detail discussion of the problem in transition see: Schmieding, H. (1993), p. 233.

Chapter 2

Basic Features of an Economy in the Transition from Plan to Market

During the transition from plan to market, especially in the gradual mode of transition, the planned economy and the market economy will co-exist for some time. During this time, the planned economic mechanism is still at work, while the market economic elements have gradually emerged. Hence, a part of the economic activities have CPE-specific features, while the other part have those of a FME (free market economy). Roughly speaking, the transition from plan to market can be seen as a process, in which the FME-specific economic activities increase and the CPE-specific activities see a relative decline. Therefore, it is of great interest to identify the major differences between the two kinds of activities from the start and to examine how they act on each other in a common economic environment. Economists and sociologists have thoroughly studied the CPE and the FME as an economic system as well as a social system[27]. We are interested only in those factors, which specify these two kinds of activities. Such factors consist of resource allocation, production co-ordination and product distribution. Here we will not undertake an empirical study to examine the fundamental features of the CPE and FME, but just outline the established results in the economical literature.

2.1 Centrally Planned Economy

Unlike the situation in the industrialised market economy, where the degree of utilisation of equipment depends first and foremost on the relation between the effective demand and the volume of the productive capacity[28], which makes demand the key element for the global behaviour of the economy, a CPE continually suffers from shortage of supply. Consequently, supply is decisive for the macro behaviour of the economy. In other words, the production capacity determines consumption and investment, and thus the growth of the CPE. Contrary to laisser-faire market economy, where prices are the result of the relationship between demand and supply, prices in a CPE are determined and controlled by a planning authority and are often served as a kind of planning instrument to carry out the political priorities of the government. These two points show the principle differences between the CPE and the FME. In the following sections we will

---

[27] Allan G. Gruchy (1985)

[28] Kalecki, Michal (1972), p.12

analyse three aspects of a CPE: the behaviour of the producer, the co-ordination and the growth mechanism.

2.1.1 Producers in CPE

According to Brown and Neuberger, centralisation is both an object and a key element of the CPE[29]. As a consequence of centralised allocation, firms in the CPE are more production units rather than free enterprises, which are able to decide independently in their own interest what and how much to produce. The scope of the activities of a firm in the CPE is greatly restricted through the central plan. The assortment and the amount of production are plan-prescribed. In most cases, firms must sell their products to a given buyer at a given price according to the central planning. In short, the output-side of the firm is strictly determined through the central plan. The input-side, such as hiring of workers and buying of raw materials, is also predetermined to a great extent through the central plan. Profit is to be transferred to the central government Firms need not keep any part of the profit because they should just maintain the „simple reproduction". All the profit will be redistributed through the central plan for „enlarged reproduction". The most important duty of a firm is to fulfil the planned targets.

Within such a restricted scope of activities, „The basic motivating force for enterprises is a strong quantity drive"[30]. What drives the firms in a FME in pursuit of profit, drives the firms in the CPE in pursuit of investment[31]. Every investor (the head of the firm) thinks, that his own production is very important for the whole economy, that it must be expanded. The general shortage situation supports this kind of thought. The desire for growth suits the object of the socialist economy, – establishing a large production capacity as a material fundament for communism, so that any wish of growth is legitimated. Furthermore, the investors identify themselves with the firms. The social status of the leader of a firm depends not only on the production capacity of the firm, but also on the number of employed workers in the firm and on the level of modernisation the firm has reached. Thus, the leaders have personal interests in the growth of the firm. Often the ability and achievement of a firm leader is judged by the amount of investment, which he is able to acquire from the planning authority. There is no direct relationship between the success of an investment project and the distribution of the investment funds. The soft-budget in CPE always guarantees some success for any investment project. In general, there is no mechanism that could hold back the desire of investment on the level of firms in CPE, so that the demand for investment tends to be „almost infinite".

---

[29]Bornstein, Morris (1974), p. 236 ff.
[30]Hare, Paul (1989), p.55.
[31]Kornai (1981), p.192

Centralisation leads to a bureaucratic working style in management and to disincentives in firms. „It is commonly assumed that technical inefficiency is ripe within centrally planned economies due to the lax discipline resulting from inadequate incentives, the absence of attention to costs due to fixation on output quota, and the hiding of output potential to avoid future increases in plan targets. Additionally, bureaucratic allocation is thought to contribute to technical inefficiency by causing subordinates to hoard input in anticipation of future shortages and to use inputs that do not fit specifications, while superiors create units of inefficient size to minimise difficulties of control."[32]

Empirical studies could not show significant evidence of a better performance of the enterprises in market economy regarding the choice of efficient technology. On the contrary, similar results concerning the efficiency of a chosen technique were found in empirical studies for both CPE and FME. This contradiction between empirical studies and common knowledge lies in the methods used in the studies. The efficiency of a chosen technology is always evaluated at given prices. The chosen technologies are efficient, only if the prices are determined according to the scarcity of the production factors. The practice of the price determination in the CPE[33] will generally not guarantee a correct evaluation of the scarcity of a product (competitive price). Thus, even the chosen „efficient technology" in the CPE are only formally rational and not efficient, as far as there is no sound price forming mechanism. This kind of formal efficiency in the CPE is also encouraged through multi-object plan targets, in which reduction of cost is one of the most important objects[34]. Hence, we can say, despite the fact that the firms in the CPE are largely restricted in the scope of their activities, they are still able to minimise their costs according to given prices.

2.1.2 The Planning Co-ordination

In a CPE the allocation of resources and the production in different enterprises is not co-ordinated through supply and demand on the market, but through central planning. The investment in the 'bottleneck' sectors is the main instrument to co-ordinate the economy. Since investment is desired by every enterprise, the financial capacity of the central planning authority becomes the sole barrier which can stop the realisation of the almost infinite demand for investment. The central planning authority has to make decisions about the investment projects according to its financial ability and available resources. The decision of the central planning

---

[32]Murell, Peter (1991), pp.63-67.
[33]For details see: Liu Zuofu and Wang Zhenzhi (1986) p 67-93. and/or Krug, Barbara (1986), p.12.
[34]Compare: Zhu Xingcheng (1984), p.35.

authority is not judged by the profitability of each project, but by some importance ranking resulting from political priorities. The changing situation on the political stage in socialist countries and its strong links to the economy make the modelling of the behaviour of the planning authority very difficult. Although there are many contributions concerning this topic[35], a sound theory on the behaviour of the planners is not yet established. The main difficulty lies in the strong ideological influence on the behaviour of the planners rather than economic considerations[36]. For simplicity, we will adopt in the model the hypotheses „allocation according to permanent proportions", postulated by Kornai from the empirical observation[37].

2.1.3 The Growth Mechanism

The growth in the CPE depends mainly on investment through the central planning. The enterprises own only enough capital as to maintain the "simple reproduction", but not the "expanded reproduction". Consumers´ savings are put into investment solely through the central planning. The planning authority makes decisions about the investment projects according to the amount of capital available. The amount of available capital depends in turn upon not only the savings of the consumers, but also up on the total profits of the enterprises. Therefore it depends upon the production capacity of the enterprises. In this way the desire for growth results in an even stronger desire for growth. Through this positive feed back a ´quantity drive´ comes into being in the CPE. In practice, the consequence of this pressure for growth is that the production of consumption goods is always pushed aside to make way for the production of investment goods. Forced savings become a typical feature in the CPEs.

Kalecki has developed a fundamental theory of growth for the CPE. While Kornai´s work is mainly concerned with the subject of the micro level in the CPE, Kalecki´s work deals with the macro phenomena in the CPE. According to Kalecki´s theory, while the problem of growth in the capitalist economy is the utilisation of the production capacity, the problem in the socialist economy is how much of the fully utilised production capacity is used for the productive accumulation or for consumption. He describes the growth problem in the socialist economy in the framework of a decision model. We may summarise Kalecki´s model as follows:

$$Y = I + L + C$$

---

[35] See:Zhou Huizhong(1993) p.561-580. and Zhou Huizhong(1992), p.456 ff.
[36] Grosfeld, Irena (1987) p.180-191.
[37] Konai (1981) p.218

Y: the national income, I: the productive investment, L: the increase in inventory, C: the consumption. $I+L$ is the productive accumulation.

Following Kalecki´s theory the increment in national income ΔY is a function of investment I and the level of the national income in a given year:[38]:

$$\Delta Y = \frac{1}{m} I - aY + uY$$

or

$$\frac{\Delta Y}{Y} = \frac{1}{m}\frac{I}{Y} - a + u$$

m: the capital-output ratio; a: the parameter of depreciation; u: the coefficient of technical and management improvement.

The increase in inventory is postulated to be proportional to the increment of the national incomes.

$$L = \mu \Delta Y$$

and

$$\frac{L}{Y} = \mu g = \mu \frac{\Delta Y}{Y}$$

The rate of the growth can thus be determined by the share of productive accumulation in the national income.

$$g = \frac{i}{\kappa} - \frac{m}{\kappa}(a-u) \quad \text{with:} \quad i = \frac{I+L}{Y} \quad \text{and} \quad \kappa = m + \mu$$

The equation above can be interpreted as a budget constrain in the decision model about the growth in the socialist economy. An increase in the productive accumulation for higher rate of growth and so a larger increment of national income in next period implies, at the same time, a decrease in the share of consumption in the national income, and so a decrease of consumption in this period. Hence, the decision is a "trade off" between growth and consumption[39] because "in the socialist system the productive capacity is, at least in principle, fully utilised."[40] This relationship between consumption and growth can be seen clearly if we

---

[38]Kalecki (1972) p.34.
[39]Chen (1990) p.67
[40]Kalecki (1972) p.35.

multiply both sides of the above equation with Y, and restate the equation in terms of consumption instead of investment.

$$gY_t + Y_t = \frac{iY_t}{\kappa} - \frac{m}{\kappa}(a-u)Y_t + Y_t$$

Inserting $(1+g)Y_t = Y_{t+1}$ and $iY_t = I_t + L_t = Y_t - C_t$ in the above equation, we get:

$$Y_{t+1} + C_t/\kappa = Y_t(1 + \frac{1}{\kappa} - \frac{m}{\kappa}(a-u)).$$

The right hand side of the above equation depends on the given production capacity in the present period, which is independent from the decision. Therefore, the total of the disposition is constrained. This decision problem can be graphically illustrated in the following way:

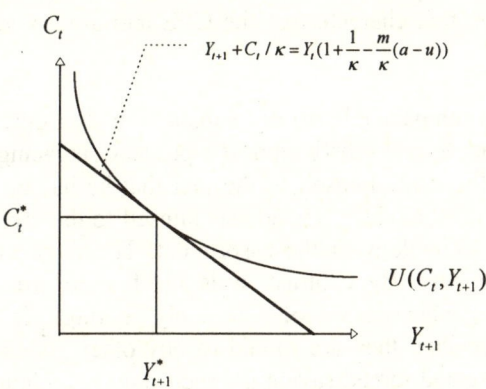

Graph 2.1 Indifference curves and budget constraint of the planning authority

Graph 2.1 above makes it clear that in the CPE the share of consumption in the national income can be used as an instrument to accelerate the rate of growth. Under the strong desire for growth –„quantity drive", the decision tends „naturally" to keep the planned share of consumption in the national income at a very low level. Moreover, this low level of consumption is even more repressed through the expansion of productive accumulation in the practice.

2.1.4 The Disequilibrium

In the literature on the CPE, shortage is the most often used term to describe the general situation of the CPE.

„The word shortage is a summary denomination of a large amount of phenomena. What comes to one's mind on hearing this word is shortage in consumer goods or housing; or queuing up in the strict sense of the word in front of the baker's or butcher's shop, it may also be notional queuing, such as waiting for the installation of telephone or admission to a hospital. Similar phenomena in production are labour shortage; or shortage of material, of parts or of electric current." „There are numerous denominations in use in economic science to the whole group of the phenomena or, at least, to one or more their significant features. The most important ones are the following: shortage economy, seller's market, repressed inflation, taut planning, overheating, over ambitious planning." Kornai stresses that "the shortage is either the reason of other phenomena or the result of them, ...It is connected by a million ties to other components of the economic system, to price, to wage, to planning and to market, to fiscal policy, to material and moral incentives. In short: Shortage is the phenomenon, that characterises the CPE and always accompanies it."

Supply shortage is always accompanied by forced substitution. Not only consumers but also producers suffer from forced substitution. If a producer is facing a resource constraint, he will not usually resign himself to the fact that he has hit a resource constraint, rather he tries to do something. He adjusts himself to the given situation. He changes his production technology or the assortment. The forced substitution reduces the shortage in no way. By contrast, it is itself an expression of the shortage. Consumers are the main victims of the supply shortage. If the desired consumer goods are not available, they are forced to buy other goods or to save their money. Forced spending and forced saving are their only two choices. Forced substitution is the spillover of the disequilibrium in the economy.

Disequilibrium in the form of supply shortage in every sector seems, at first glance, contradictory to Walras´ law. Actually, excess demand is supported through forced saving of consumers and the soft-budget of firms in the CPE. The soft-budget enables firms to claim investment goods beyond their budget constraints. At the same time, forced saving, which results from the shortage of supply of consumer goods, provides the financial capital for investment through the centrally controlled banking system. Thus, forced saving closes the financing deficit between realised and planned investment. Produced investment goods, hence, can always be sold, even if the planned financial endowment is insufficient.

In the empirical studies on the CPE, Portes and Quandt[41] analysed CPEs in the framework of a disequilibrium model. They describe the phenomena, which Kornai calls shortage, in terms of disequilibrium. In their contributions, the existence of a disequilibrium was postulated and estimated according to the empirical observations. There exists some controversy among the different schools about the theoretical approaches to the CPE[42]. The discussions focused mainly on, which model is more adequate to describe the phenomena in the CPE. The existence of disequilibrium is commonly accepted.

2.2 Market Economy

Theories about the market economy are much more advanced than those about the planned economy. Economical theories cover almost every different topic in the market economy. In this manuscript, we are interested in the market economy as an organisation in its classical form. During the emergence of the market segment in the planned economy, the participants in the market are rather small and poorly organised. The classical theory provides an adequate description of market activities. Moreover, the classical theory, with „laisser faire" and „invisible hand" as its principle components, is more or less the main image of the market economy which the reform policy-makers were pursuing. The price mechanism acts as the strongest force in the co-ordination of the market activities. In the following section we are going to analyse the FME in two aspects: the market co-ordination and the growth mechanism.

2.2.1 The Market Co-ordination

The centre piece of the classic theory on the market economy is competitive equilibrium. In the theoretical model, the actors of the economy are producers and consumers. They behave rationally and pursue maximal profit and maximal utility respectively. The market can co-ordinate these decentralised decisions of the actors through an „invisible hand".

Producers

The Producers in market economy make decisions independently concerning production, price, and the choice of technology. They are responsible for the success or failure resulting from their decision. The profit belongs to the producer, who also has to take the risk of loss. Every producer operates anonymously on the

---

[41] Davis and Charemza (1989), p.27-48 p.147-178.
[42] Davis and Charemza (1989), p.3-25.

market. He tries to maximise his own profit against the competition on the market. Since every producer can make decisions independently, production in the market economy is flexible and the allocation of resources reacts to the market situation. Demand plays an important role in the economy. It is taken into account in the decision of producers. Hence, demand is one of the determinants of the equilibrium in market economy, not as in the planned economy, where demand, being the short side of disequilibrium, is almost always latent.

Consumers

Refer to the behaviour principle of consumers, it does not make any difference whether consumers get their income from a state-owned enterprise or from a private one[43]. They try to maximise their utility within their budget constraints. Of course, in the centrally planned economy, consumers, as they are constrained by the shortage of supply, might appear to have another consumer behaviour. As is generally known, the realised consumption in this disequilibrium situation is not the notional consumption demand, i.e. what the consumer would really buy if there were no supply constraint. The spillover of the supply shortage is forced substitution or forced saving. Hence, the notional demand becomes latent. During the transition, consumers in the economy face the same supply situation – with the supply from the market segment and the supply from the planned segment. It is, therefore, reasonable to assume that they have the same behaviour, irrespective of whether their income comes from the planned segment or the market segment.

Market

Equilibrium is an essential feature of market economy if the small market participants are co-ordinated through the market mechanism – the flexible price and the decentralised allocation of resource. Supply and demand are kept equal. According to the theory of general equilibrium, economy is in a pareto optimum and the allocation of resources is efficient[44].

2.2.2 The Growth Mechanism

Unlike in the CPE in which the growth rate, or more precisely, the rate of capital accumulation is determined by the planning authority, the growth rate in the market economy is the result of market equilibrium. The growth of economy may be understood as the growth of production, which depends mainly on investment. The realised investment in each period is in turn the result of the equilibrium in which

---

[43]See Portes (1989), p.27
[44]Compare: Varian (1981)

not only supply but also demand determine the total realised investment. The factor pricing, the factor income and the saving behaviour, therefore, are all relevant to growth. All temporary equilibria in each period together constitute the growth path of the system.

2.3 Economy in Transition from Plan to Market

The economy during the transition from plan to market may be viewed as a mixture of CPE and FME. There are producers who are integrated in the plan system. The planning procedure is still functional in some way. These producers have to fulfil the prescribed plan targets. Their products are sold at the plan price. The behaviour of these producers have the CPE specific pattern. We call these producers the „planned segment". Beside the producers in the planned segment, there also exist enterprises which operate fully independently according to the market principle. Their products are dealt on the „market" at market prices. We call them the „market segment". Consumers can buy goods from market suppliers as well as plan suppliers.

If the shares in this mixture change in favour of market, a transition takes place. In this context, we should distinguish between two kinds of changes during the transition from plan to market. The first one is the quantitative expansion of the market segment. This may be the increment in the number of free enterprises or the enlargement of the production of existing free enterprises. At any rate, this kind of change contributes to transition through the growth of the production capacity in the market segment, where producers are originally market-specific. We call this kind of transition an extrinsic transition. The other kind is the change in the plan segment, where the behaviour of producers becomes increasingly market-like due to reforms and adjustments to the new situation in the economy. The amount of planned target may gradually reduce. The plan price adjustment responds more and more to the demand and supply on the market. This kind of change contributes to the transition through market-orienting adjustment in the plan segment. We call it an intrinsic transition.

Methodically the extrinsic transition can be best described as a growth process within a conventional neo-classic equilibrium framework as the driving force of the extrinsic transition is the expansion of the market segment in the economy. The expansion of the market segment depends mainly on the real investment in the market segment. The real investment depends in turn on factors such as saving behaviour, distribution of factor income, the demand for investment, and the price level, which are all co-ordinated through market mechanism. Since the neo-classic theory of growth provides a proper formal structure for modelling the market mechanism in a growth process, the extrinsic transition can be well captured in this framework. It is much more difficult to describe the intrinsic transition in a formal model structure. The intrinsic transition covers topics such as change in the environment of the state-owned enterprises, the transformation of state-owned enterprises and the privatization of the state-owned enterprises, the change in the performance of state-owned enterprises, the change of the factor allocation mechanism in the planned segment, and the capital outflow from the planned segment into the market segment. There is still no sound theory on these phenomena. The main difficulty lies in the subjective character of the reform policy-making and the turbulent features of the transformation from the deconstruction of the old economic structure to the reconstruction of a new one. The overall state of the economic system during the transition depends on which type of transitional form plays a dominant role in the system. If the extrinsic transition is the dominant one, the overall transition process will be a smooth process, which can be properly described in the framework of a growth model. If the intrinsic transition plays the governing role, the system behaviour will be turbulent, according to the chosen policies.

Most of the current literature about the transition from plan to market focuses on the transition topics in the sense of intrinsic transition. There are many unsolved theoretical problems concerning this form of transition[45]. These problems hinder the theory from providing a good travel guide for the reform policy-makers to find their way successfully to a market economy.

In the Chinese mode of transition — growing out of plan, the extrinsic transition dominating the overall transition process, the growth of the market segment has been the main driving force of the transition from plan to market. The intrinsic transition may be viewed as an adjustment of the planned segment to the challenge from the market situation. The „two-tiers system" was designed to enable the state-owned enterprises to get more involved in the market and the price reform was intended to give the state-owned enterprises an equal chance in the competition on the market. Hence, the transition process in China as modelled in this thesis is a growth process within an equilibrium framework. The intrinsic transition is treated as an impact of the exogenous policy-making on the system. As the extrinsic transition is the direct result of the market forces, the intrinsic transition is indirectly driven by market forces. Thus, the transition from plan to market may be described by the decreasing share of the planned segment in the whole economy, and the adjustment, or more precisely the forced adjustment, of the planned segment to the market situation.

---

[45] For details see: Holger Schmieding (1993), p.216-53 ff and Peter Murrell (1991) p. 59-75.

Chapter 3

A Theoretical Model for Transition Process

3.1 General Approach

To model the transition from plan to market we have to capture elements which express plan activities and market activities in the model, and we should describe the changes of these two elements within the system. One important aspect is to distinguish the two different kinds of changes – the intrinsic transition and the extrinsic transition- and to treat them differently according to the cause of these two kinds of changes. The extrinsic transition, which is carried out through the quantitative expansion of the market, can be adequately described through the growth process of the market economic activities. To model the intrinsic transition, which depends on the qualitative change of the behaviour in the planned economic system, we must consider the political instrumental character of the intrinsic transition. Owing to the influence of subjectivity in this kind of change, we will treat the intrinsic transition exogenously and discuss the impact of these exogenous changes on the whole system.

Another aspect specific to the Chinese economy is the consideration of the influence of the industrialisation process on the transition from plan to market. The industrialisation process in China, stimulated by economic reform, coincided with the transition from plan to market. This is one of the most important reasons why the transition process in China differs from those in east European countries[46]. As described in chapter one, the transition from plan to market in China is accompanied, or more precisely, promoted through the decentralised industrialisation process. The decentralised industrialisation is itself much favoured by the liberal economic environment during the reform. The impact of the industrialisation process is too huge to be neglected in the modelling of the transition process from plan to market.

One approach to the construction of a formal model is to capture in a single framework features which are relevant for the two processes. However, each of the two processes is in itself a very complex economic phenomenon. An all-around consideration would make it very difficult, if not impossible, to study the behaviour of the system analytically.

---

[46]Similar conclusion is obtained by Schmieding: From plan to market: on the nature of the transition crisis, Weltwirtschaftliches Archiv 1994 p.244

To avoid this sort of difficulty, we will merely consider the most important features of the CPE and the FME and incorporate them in a theoretical model, in which a dualistic structure prevails. The model is thus constructed in two segments, the planned segment and the market segment, and two sectors, industry and agriculture. This two by two division provides a convenient framework to outline the transition process and the industrialisation process, as well as the relation between these two processes. The transition from plan to market is described as the change of the relative weight of the two economic segments in the whole economy. The industrialisation process is expressed through the increasing share of industrial products in the total production.

At the outset, there already exists a certain productive capacity in the planned economic segment. This subsystem can be taken as an independent economic sub-system, in the sense that it can function on its own with complete functions of the resource allocation, the co-ordination of production and the distribution of products. This subsystem bears the basic features of a CPE:

1) The prices in this segment are fixed (determined by the planning authority).
2) There exists no equilibrium in this segment.
3) The production structure is rigid (shares of investment products and consumer products do not react to the demand situation).

The market economic segment, contrary to the planned economic segment, is a newly emerged subsystem. Its productive capacity is relatively small at the beginning. At the outset, it is not an independent economic sub-system and has to rely on exchange with the planned economic segment. But the functioning of this subsystem carries the basic features of a FME:

1) The producers are the price-takers and are in pursuit of maximal profits under the given conditions on the market.
2) The prices respond to the demand and the supply on the market and thus keep supply and demand in balance.
3) The allocation of resources is determined according to supply and demand on the market.

We consider the economy as a closed one[47] with an agricultural and an industrial sector, each of which produces a homogenous commodity. The output of agricultural good is only consumed. The industrial output may be consumed or

---

[47]Through the assumption of a closed economy we neglect the impact of international trade and foreign investment on the transition and industrialisation process. The importance of international trade and foreign on the industrialisation can be seen in Perkins (1994).

invested[48]. We assume that the economy consists of labourers, who supply only labour services, capitalists, who supply no labour service but are the owners of the productive means in the economy, and the state, which owns the productive units in the planned segment.

3.2 The Planned Economic Segment

Production Technology

The production technology in the model is assumed to be neo-classic and expressed by a neo-classic production function. There are two homogeneous production factors, namely labour and capital. The production function is assumed to be twice differentiable and single valued with a constant return of scale[49].

$$Y_{iP} = F^i(K_{iP}, L_{iP}) \tag{1p}$$

with: i = 1 denotes the agricultural sector.
i = 2 denotes the industrial sector.
The subscript P denote the planned segment
L_{iP}: labour used in i-th sector of the planned segment
K_{iP}: capital used in i-th sector of the planned segment
Y_{iP}: production of the i-th sector of the planned segment

The first partial differentials are supposed to be positive: $F^i_{K_{iP}}{}'(K_{iP}, L_{iP}) > 0$; $F^i_{L_{iP}}{}'(K_{iP}, L_{iP}) > 0$ and the second differentials negative: $F^i_{K_{iP}}{}''(K_{iP}, L_{iP}) < 0$; $F^i_{L_{iP}}{}''(K_{iP}, L_{iP}) < 0$.

At the very beginning, the technological progress is not considered because the main interest lies in the analysis of the interaction between the two segments, which can be traced back institutionally but not technologically. Considering the special situation in China, we assume the agricultural production takes place only in the market segment but not the planned segment. The influence of planning on the agriculture will be discussed later. The following terms, therefore, are equal to zero: $K_{1P} = 0$, $L_{1P} = 0$ and $Y_{1P} = 0$.

---

[48] In the development-theoretical literature by Fei and Ranis and Jorgenson the industrial output is admitted for both consumption and investment purposes.
[49] Non-constant return to scale has weakness in growth model, see Conlisk 1968.

The total industrial production consists of the production of investment goods and the production of consumption goods.

$$Y_{2P} = I_{2P} + C_{2P} \qquad (2p)$$

Planner's Decision about factor demand

We assume that the decision about production in the planned segment is made by a planner, who is interested in reaching maximal production in the future. Because labour supply always exists there (see 3.3), the planner's decision for the maximal production in the future is equivalent to a decision for maximal investment in each foregoing period. We assume that the price and the wage rate are fixed. The decision problem can be described as follows:

$$Max: I_{2P}^P = F^2(K_{2P}, L_{2P}) - C_{2P}^P$$
r.t.:
$$K_{2P} \leq K_P$$
$$P_{2P} C_{2P}^P \geq w_P L_{2P}$$

The first restriction says that the capital stock is bounded. The second restriction means the planner has to consider providing a certain amount of consumption goods for the labourers in the planned segment, where all the labour incomes are assumed to be used for consumption[50]. Obviously, the maximum will be reached when the two restrictions are realised as equations. Hence, we can put the restrictions in the object function and solve them.

$$\frac{\partial F^2}{\partial L_{2P}} = \frac{w_P}{P_{2P}} \qquad (3p)[51]$$

$$K_{2P} = K_P$$

Noting that, (3p) can also be interpreted as a cost-minimising condition, thus we will refer this to cost-minimising behaviour of the producer in the later discussion. From (3p) we get the demand for labour as the function of the real wage rate and the capital stock.

---

[50] We will discuss the case of saving from labour income in chapter 5. See also Marglin (1984) „Growth, Distribution and Prices,, p.53.
[51] We have this condition from the maximising behaviour of the planner. It especially suits the case before the economic reform. But this condition also implies cost minimising behaviour, if the price and the wage rate are kept fixed.

$$L_{2P} = L_{2P}(K_{2P}, \frac{w_P}{P_{2P}}) \qquad (3p\text{-}b)$$

Because $K_{2P} = K_P$ always holds, we will later consider only K_{2P}. The capital stock at each period is the past level minus depreciation plus investment:

$$K_{2P}(t) = K_{2P}(t-1) + I_P^P(t) - \delta K_{2P}(t-1)$$

Capital Payment

The capital payment can be determined residually as the difference between the whole income and the labour payment.

$$r_P K_P = r_P K_{2P} = P_{2P} Y_{2P} - w_P L_{2P}$$

The rental rate of capital can be calculated accordingly:

$$r_P = \frac{P_{2P} Y_{2P} - w_P L_{2P}}{K_{2P}} \qquad (4p)$$

Commodity Market

Demand in the traditional CPE is always latent and plays no effective role in the economy. While the market segment emerges in the economy, demand, which is originally kept latent through supply constraint, can now be articulated on the free market. Concerning the disposition of income, we make the assumption of the classical saving behaviour[52]. We assume that labour incomes will all be consumed and that the saving fraction of capital income is s_r and that the savings will be directly used for investment by the planner. Thus we get nominal demand for consumption from the planned segment:

$$NC_P^d = w_P L_P + (1 - s_r) r_P K_P, \qquad (5p)$$

and nominal demand for investment from the planned segment:

$$NI_P^d = s_r r_P K_P. \qquad (6p)$$

As discussed in chapter 2, the practice in the planned economy leads to a shortage of supply for consumption. The determination of the realised share of investment goods and consumer goods in the total production is a very complicated matter, in which the ideological doctrine and economic calculation as well as the bureaucratic practice are entangled. To simplify this complication, we

---

[52]Marglin (1984): Growth, Distribution and Prices p.111.

adopt Kornai's hypothesis of the „permanent proportion"[53] and take the ratio between the investment and consumption as an exogenous variable (7p).

$$\frac{I_{2P}}{C_{2P}} = \mu \qquad (7p)$$

We assume that the realised supply of consumption can not be larger than demand so that the difference between demand and supply is always positive. We can take this difference between the nominal demand and nominal supply as a measurement of the disequilibrium and denote it as E:

$$E = NC_P^d - P_{2P}C_{2P} \qquad (8p)$$

or

$$E = P_{2P}I_{2P} - NI_P^d \qquad (8p\text{-}b)$$

At first glance, the equation (8p-b) seems to be an excess supply of the investment good, which would be contradictory to the specific features of CPE, where there are shortages of supply in every sector as described in chapter two. The almost infinite demand for investment goods means that the produced investment goods can always be sold. Under the soft budget constraint the investor does not pay much attention to budget constraint. The spillover of the shortage of supply of consumer goods, i.e. forced saving, can, through the central planning, just cover the financial deficit expressed in (8p-b). In the planned economic segment the willingness for investment is everywhere, as in a CPE[54]. The realised investment depends only on the financial capability of the planning authority. If forced saving exists, the total amount of investment is equal to the sum of the capital income and the forced saving. It should be noted that forced saving and the financially uncovered investment demands take place at the same time. It is not forced saving that causes the infinite demand for investment. By contrast, the quantity drive causes the over-evaluation of investment, which results in insufficient production of consumer goods and forced saving.

3.3 Market Economic Segment

Production Technology

Similar to the planned economic segment, the production technology in the market segment is assumed to be expressed through the same production function,

---

[53] Kornai (1980): „Economics of Shortage", p.218 ff.
[54] Jefferson, Gary H. and Rawski Thomas G. (1994): p.55

$$Y_{iM} = F^i(K_{iM}, L_{iM}) \qquad (1m\text{-}2m)$$

with:
> The subscript M denote the market segment
> K_{iM} : capital stock i-th sector of the market segment
> L_{iM}: labour used in i-th sector of the market segment
> Y_{iM}: production of the i-th sector of the market segment

The first partial differentials are assumed to be positive: $F'_{K_{iM}}(K_{iM}, L_{iM}) > 0$, $F'_{L_{iM}}(K_{iM}, L_{iM}) > 0$ and the second differentials to be negative $F''_{K_{iM}}(K_{iM}, L_{iM}) < 0$, $F''_{L_{iM}}(K_{iM}, L_{iM}) < 0$. Thus, each sector is analogous to a large firm and exhibiting optimal behaviour, which implies cost minimising with respect to inputs and revenue maximisation with respect to outputs. The assumption of identical production technology in both segments is supported by the fact that all feasible technology is accessible to producers in both segments.

Industrial production consists of production of investment goods and consumption goods:

$$Y_{2M} = I_{2M} + C_{2M} \qquad (3m)$$

Factor Market

The total capital stock in the market segment at period t is denoted as $K_M(t)$ and will be fully utilised in the two sectors.

$$K_M(t) = K_{1M}(t) + K_{2M}(t) \qquad (4m)$$

At the given period t, the total capital stock is determined by the level of last period plus the net investment:

$$K_M(t) = K_M(t-1) + I_M^m(t) - \delta K_M(t-1)$$

It is assumed that the capital adjusts instantaneously to any price difference between sectors and that there are no costs associated with the transfer. This assumption is based on the observation that factor adjustments to price discrepancies will take much less time than the transition process and the industrialisation process.

We assume that the allocation of factors is efficient and the factors are paid at their marginal value products. That is, the factor combinations fulfil the minimum cost condition:

$$\frac{\partial F^i}{\partial K_{iM}} = \frac{r_{iM}}{P_{iM}} \qquad i=1,2 \qquad (5m\text{-}6m)$$

$$\frac{\partial F^i}{\partial L_{iM}} = \frac{w_{iM}}{P_{iM}} \qquad i=1,2 \qquad (7m\text{-}8m)$$

As in the planned economic segment, the labour demand can be expressed as a function of the capital stock and the real wage rate in this segment:

$$L_{iM} = L_{iM}(K_{iM}, \frac{w_{iM}}{P_{iM}}).$$

The total employed labour is the sum of the labour employed in the two sectors.

$$L_M = L_{1M} + L_{2M}. \qquad (9m)$$

We assume that all the surplus labour force will be absorbed in agriculture. Therefore:

$$L_M + L_{2P} = L_G \qquad (10m)$$

Because the production function has a constant return of scale, the total income can be divided into capital income and labour income:

$$P_{iM} Y_{iM} = w_{iM} L_{iM} + r_{iM} K_{iM}$$

Accordingly, the rental rate of capital can be determined as follows:

$$r_{iM} = \frac{P_{iM} Y_{iM} - w_{iM} L_{iM}}{K_{iM}}$$

We assume that the capital movement within the market segment is subject to no institutional constraints and is, therefore, much more flexible. The capital movement will cease if the rental rates are equal in both sectors.

$$r_{1M} = r_{2M} = r_M. \qquad (11m)$$

The total capital income and the total labour income are the sum of those incomes, respectively, in both sectors:

$$r_M K_M = r_M (K_{1M} + K_{2M})$$

$$w_M L_M = w_{1M} L_{1M} + w_{2M} L_{2M}$$

Wages and Labour

In the model, we assume that the nominal wage rate in the industrial sector is determined by the government through institutional regulation. The difference between the nominal wages in the market segment and the planned segment lies mainly in the payment of social services such as health insurance, retirement payments, housing subsidies, pay in kind, etc. Therefore, we assume that there is an exogenously determined relation between the nominal wage rates in both segments.

$$w_{2M} = v_E w_P \quad \text{with} \quad v_E \leq 1 \tag{12m}$$

Due to the dualistic structure of the economy, there is a large labour force willing to work in the industrial sector because the wage rate in the industry is higher than that of agriculture, at least at the beginning of the transition process. This tendency of labour movement leads to that the real wage rate can not increase until the surplus labour supply for industry disappears. This minimum level can be seen as a kind of existence minimum in the urban area. The rigidity of the minimum level of the real wage can be described by a wage function[55], where the nominal wage is tied to the prices in a certain relationship. We assume, that the influence of agricultural products is negligible in the determination of the consumption level for the industrial workers. Hence, the minimum wage can be written as follows:

$$w_{2M} = W(P_{2P}, P_{2M}).$$

Furthermoer, we assume that there is no money illusion. The wage functions become linearly homogenous in prices. In our case, there are two prices for the same product. The minimum wage condition takes the following form:

$$w_{2M} = \delta_E (\lambda P_{2P} + (1-\lambda) P_{2M}). \tag{13m}$$

λ is the weight of the product from the planned segment in the whole economy. This wage function simply says that the nominal wage is proportional to the average price for the industrial products, which is expressed by $\lambda P_{2P} + (1-\lambda) P_{2M}$. δ_E is the minimum level of consumption per capita. From the definition of λ, we get:

---

[55] For the use of wage function see: Motoshige Itoh and Takashi Negishi, (1987) p.6.

$$\lambda = \frac{Y_{2P}}{Y_{2P} + Y_{2M}}$$

Thus the minimum wage condition can be written as:

$$\frac{w_M}{\delta_E} = \frac{Y_{2P}}{Y_{2P} + Y_{2M}}(P_{2P} - P_{2M}) + P_{2M}$$

or

$$Y_{2M}(P_{2M} - \frac{w_{2M}}{\delta_E}) = (\frac{w_{2M}}{\delta_E} - P_{2P})Y_{2P}.$$

Demand

For the agricultural product, we assume an inelastic demand:[56]

$$Y_{1M}^d = \varepsilon L_G. \tag{14m}$$

ε is the amount of food needed per capita.

For the disposition of labour income and capital income, we may make a similar assumption as we have done for the planned segment. Thus the nominal demand for consumption is:

$$NC_M^d = w_{1M}L_{1M} + w_{2M}L_{2M} + (1 - s_r)r_M K_M \tag{15m}$$

The nominal demand for investment is:

$$NI_M^d = s_r r_M K_M \tag{16m}$$

3.4 Market Balance

For a pure market economy it is quite natural to accept the conception of equilibrium, as suggested by the general equilibrium theory. In the case of an economy with two segments, the question is whether the market economic segment can absorb the disequilibrium effect resulting from the existence of the planned economic segment and keep the total demand and total supply in equilibrium. An intuitive answer would be that it depends on the relative weight of the planned segment in the whole economy. If the weight of the planned segment is very small, there would be an equilibrium. If the weight is too large, there would be no equilibrium. The existence of the planned economic segment

---

[56] More general assumption about the demand for agricultural products would be that after reaching a certain level(ε), the expenditure for agricultural products takes a small and decreasing share in the total consumption expenditure. Compare. Kelly et al (1972) p.44 ff.

affects through the deficit in supply expressed by E. If production and prices of the market segment are flexible enough so that they can cover this deficit, then there will be equilibrium. If the deficit can not be covered by the production of the market segment, there will be no equilibrium and forced saving and forced substitution exist. The condition of equilibrium can be put as follows:

$$Y_{1M}^d = Y_{1M} \tag{17m}$$

$$P_{2M}I_{2M} = NI_M^d - E \tag{18m}$$

$$P_{2M}C_{2M} = NC_M^d - P_{1M}Y_{1M} + E \tag{19m}$$

According to Walras' law, one of the three equations is dependent on the other two, so we only need to study two of them. This equilibrium condition can be understood as follows: The existence of the planned segment results in a deficit of supply for consumer goods in the planned segment. The market force adjusts the production and the price for the consumer goods in the market segment so that this deficit is closed. At the same time, supply and demand for the investment good is also brought into balance.

3.5 Special Features of the Model

All in all, the whole model consists of 31 variables with 26 independent equations and 5 exogenous variables. The following is a list of the variables:

List of variables

1	P_{2P}	planned price for industrial goods	exogenous
2	w_P	planned wage rate	exogenous
3	K_{2P}	capital stock in the industrial sector of the planned segment	exogenous
4	L_{2P}	employed labour in the industrial sector of the planned segment	endogenous
5	I_{2P}	the amount of produced investment goods	endogenous
6	C_{2P}	the amount of produced consumer goods	endogenous
7	Y_{2P}	the amount of industrial products	endogenous
8	r_P	the rental rate in the planned economic segment	endogenous
9	NC_P^d	demand for consumption from the planned segment	endogenous
10	NI_P^d	demand for investment from the planned segment	endogenous

11	E	shortage of supply for consumer goods in planned segment	endogenous
12	K_{1M}:	capital stock in the agricultural sector	endogenous
13	K_{2M}	capital stock in the industrial sector of the market segment	endogenous
14	P_{1M}	market price for the agricultural goods	endogenous
15	P_{2M}	market price for the industrial goods	endogenous
16	L_{1M}	labour employed in the agricultural sector	endogenous
17	L_{2M}	labour employed in the industrial sector of the market segment	endogenous
18	L_M	total labour employed in the market segment	endogenous
19	Y_{1M}	amount of agricultural goods produced in the market segment	endogenous
20	Y_{2M}	amount of industrial goods produced in the market segment	endogenous
21	r_{1M}	rental rate of capital in the agricultural sector	endogenous
22	r_{2M}	rental rate of capital in the industrial sector	endogenous
23	K_M	total capital stock in the market segment	exogenous
24	w_{2M}	market wage rate in the industrial sector	endogenous
25	w_{1M}	market wage rate in the agricultural sector	endogenous
26	I_{2M}	produced investment goods in the market segment	endogenous
27	C_{2M}	produced consumer goods in the market segment	endogenous
28	Y_1^d	demand for the agricultural products	endogenous
29	NC_M^d	nominal demand for consumption from the market segment	endogenous
30	NI_M^d	nominal demand for investment from the market segment	endogenous
31	L_G	total labour force	exogenous

Summary of equations:

1) Equations for the planned segment:

$$Y_{2P} = F^2(K_{iP}, L_{iP}) \qquad (1p)$$

$$Y_{2P} = I_{2P} + C_{2P} \qquad (2p)$$

$$\frac{\partial F_{2P}}{\partial L_{2P}} = \frac{w_P}{P_{2P}} \qquad (3p)$$

$$r_P = \frac{P_{2P}Y_{2P} - w_P L_{2P}}{K_{2P}} \tag{4p}$$

$$NC_P^d = w_P L_P + (1 - s_r) r_P K_P, \tag{5p}$$

$$NI_P^d = s_r r_P K_P. \tag{6p}$$

$$\frac{I_{2P}}{C_{2P}} = \mu \tag{7p}$$

$$E = NC_P^d - P_{2P} C_{2P} \tag{8p}$$

2) Equations for the market segment:

$$Y_{iM} = F^i(K_{iM}, L_{iM}) \tag{1m-2m}$$

$$Y_{2M} = I_{2M} + C_{2M} \tag{3m}$$

$$K_M(t) = K_{1M}(t) + K_{2M}(t) \tag{4m}$$

$$\frac{\partial F_{iM}}{\partial K_{iM}} = \frac{r_{iM}}{P_{iM}} \tag{5m-6m}$$

$$\frac{\partial F_{iM}}{\partial L_{iM}} = \frac{w_{iM}}{P_{iM}} \tag{7m-8m}$$

$$L_M = L_{1M} + L_{2M} \tag{9m}$$

$$L_M + L_{2P} = L_G \tag{10m}$$

$$r_{1M} = r_{2M} = r_M \tag{11m}$$

$$w_{2M} = v_E w_P \tag{12m}$$

$$w_{2M} = \delta_E(\lambda P_{2P} + (1-\lambda) P_{2M}). \tag{13m}$$

$$Y_{1M}^d = \varepsilon L_G. \tag{14m}$$

$$NC_M^d = w_{1M} L_{1M} + w_{2M} L_{2M} + (1 - s_r) r_M K_M \tag{15m}$$

$$NI_M^d = s_r r_M K_M \tag{16m}$$

$$Y_{1M}^d = Y_{1M} \qquad (17m)$$

$$P_{2M}I_{2M} = NI_M^d + NI_P^d - P_{2P}I_{2P} \qquad (18m)$$

$$P_{2M}C_{2M} = NC_M^d + NC_P^d - P_{2P}C_{2P} - P_{1M}Y_{1M} \qquad (19m)$$

3) Equations for the dynamic properties of the system:

$$K_{2P}(t) = K_{2P}(t-1) + I_P^P(t) - \delta K_{2P}(t-1) \qquad (A)$$

$$K_M(t) = K_M(t-1) + I_M^m(t) - \delta K_M(t-1) \qquad (B)$$

$I_M^m(t), I_P^p(t)$: real investment in the market segment and planned segment.

The Relative Independence of the Planned Segment

The activities in the planned segment are described by 8 equations and 11 variables with 3 exogenous variables, which can be taken as political instrumental variables in the planned segment. Hence, the static property in the planned segment is independent from the activities in the market segment. This independence expresses in certain ways the inflexibility of the planned economy, where the production does not react to the demand but rather depends on technology and the planning instruments.

From equation (8p) it is obvious that the shortage of supply has the same growth rate as the production. Thus it becomes clear that (7p) implies an identical rate of growth in the planned segment as long as the planning instruments remain unchanged.

The transaction between the planned segment and the market segment is modelled through the demand side. Producers from both planned and market segments have the same opportunity to obtain products from the planned and market segment. The influence of the market segment on the planned segment is carried out through the transaction between the two segments. The market segment can obtain products from the planned segment at a lower price – the plan price, – while the planned segment has to pay a higher price – the market price,– to get the products from the market segment.

The Dualistic Structure in the Market Segment

The economic activities of the market segment are described by 18 independent equations and 20 variables, two of which are exogenous. The market mechanism is manifested in the flexible price and flexible resource allocation. The exogenous variables are the resource constraints.

The dualistic structure of the economy is modelled in the following three aspects: production technology, demand and labour distribution. The agricultural production is assumed to be more labour intensive. We have assumed an inelastic demand for agricultural products. Furthermore, we have assumed that the wage rate in the industrial sector lies above the competitive level and it draws labour from agriculture to industry. But the level of employment in the industry is restricted by the cost-minimising behaviour of the producers. All the remaining labour force has to be absorbed in agricultur.

3.6 Equilibrium

We say the economic system is in equilibrium, if some positive prices P_{1M} and P_{2M} exist so that the equations of market balance (18m), (19m), and (20m) can be fulfilled. That means market prices can keep the total demand and total supply for agricultural products and industrial products in balance.

The basic structure of this model can be described as follows: the planned segment, with a price rigidity and inflexible production structure, is in itself never balanced. Therefore, the planned segment can be taken as a „disturbance segment", which produces distortion in the economy. The market segment, driven by market forces, tries to correct this distortion and moves the economy to an equilibrium with it´s flexible price and flexible allocation of the production capacity. This kind of equilibrium differs from the normal concept of general equilibrium as there are two different prices for the same good, and only a part of the allocation of the resource responds to the market situation.

Chapter 4

Existence and Uniqueness of the Equilibrium and Dynamics of the System

4.1 Restatement of the Model

The model constructed in the last chapter consists of two segments. In solving for equilibrium we only have to consider the market segment, because the variables in the planned segment are determined through planning decisions and can be hence treated independently from the market. Owing to the constant returns to scale technology, we can restate the sub-model of the market segment in intensive form. For this purpose, we define the following new variables:

$f_i = \dfrac{F^i(K_{iM}, L_{iM})}{K_{iM}}$ capital productivity of the i-th sector in the market segment

$l_i = \dfrac{L_{iM}}{K_{iM}}$ the labour intensity of the i-th sector in the market segment

$u_i = \dfrac{K_{iM}}{K_M}$ the share of the capital in i-th sector in the market segment

With the newly defined variables, the production function can be restated in terms of labour intensity as follows:

$$F^i(K_{iM}, L_{iL}) = K_{iM} F^i(1, L_{iM}/K_{iM}) = K_{iM} F_{iM}(1, l_i) = K_{iM} f_i(l_i)$$

The differential of the above equation is:

$$F^i_{L_{iM}} = K_{iM} f_i'(l_i)/K_{iM} = f_i'(l_i)$$

For the linear homogenous production function, the Eule-Theorem holds (for convenience we have omitted the subscript):

$$F = F_K' K + F_L' L \qquad \text{or} \qquad f(l) = F_K + l f'(l)$$

Dividing both sides by f and using the relation $f' = F_L$ and $F_K/f' = F_K/F_L = r/w$, we get the following relations, respectively, for agricultural production:

$$f_1/f_1' - l_1 = \dfrac{r_M}{w_{1M}} \qquad\qquad (1ma)$$

and for industrial production:

$$f_2/f_2' - l_2 = \frac{r_M}{w_{2M}}.$$ (2ma)

The equation for market balance on the agriculture market (17m) can be written as follows:

$$u_1 f_1 = \varepsilon L_G / K_M = \varepsilon l_G$$ (3ma)

$$\text{with } u_1 = \frac{K_{1M}}{K_M} \quad \text{and} \quad l_G = \frac{L_G}{K_M}.$$

u_1 is the share of the capital stock used in the agricultural sector. u_2 is the share of the capital stock used in the industrial sector. The shares in both sectors add up to one.

$$u_1 + u_2 = 1.$$ (4ma)

Using $E = -(NI_P^d - P_{2P}I_{2P})$ and $I_{2M} = \eta_1 Y_{2M} = \eta_1 K_{2M} f_2 = \eta_1 u_2 K_M f_2$, we can rewrite the market balance for investment products (18m) as follows (here we assume $s_r = 1$):

$$\eta_1 u_2 f_2 P_{2M} = r_M - e$$ (5ma)

$$\text{with } \eta_1 = \frac{I_{2M}}{Y_{2M}} \quad \text{and} \quad e = \frac{E}{K_M}$$

η_1 is the share of investment products in the whole industrial production. η_2 is the share of consumption products in the whole industrial production. For the shares of investment goods and consumption goods the following equation holds:

$$\eta_1 + \eta_2 = 1.$$ (6ma)

From equations (7m) and (8m) we get

$$P_{1M} = \frac{w_{1M}}{f_1'}$$ (7ma)

and

$$P_{2M} = \frac{w_{2M}}{f_2'}.$$ (8ma)

We can put the full employment condition as follows:

$$l_1 u_1 + l_2 u_2 = l_M = L_M / K_M. \tag{9ma}$$

The minimum-wage condition (13m) can be restated with the new variables:

$$u_2 f_2 (P_{2M} - \frac{w_{2M}}{\delta_E}) = \frac{Y_{2P}}{K_M}(\frac{w_{2M}}{\delta_E} - P_{2P}) \tag{10ma}$$

For the nominal wage we merely restate the equation (12m):

$$w_{2M} = v_E w_P \tag{11ma}$$

In this restated system there are 11 independent equations and 11 endogenous variables: $l_1, l_2, u_1, u_2, \delta_1, \delta_2, P_{1M}, P_{2M}, w_{1M}, w_{2M}$ and r_M. Obviously the solution for this restated system is the equilibrium solution of the original system. In the next section we will answer the question, whether or not a solution for this restated system exists.

4.2 Existence and Uniqueness

The existence of a solution for the system is demonstrated in the following way. First we show that all the endogenous variables except r_M and w_{2M} can be uniquely expressed as functions of the rental wage ratio r_M / w_{2M} through the equations from (1ma) to (9ma). In the equation (10ma) an equilibrium rental wage ratio can be uniquely determined.

It is easy to show that in equations (1ma) and (2ma) a monotone relation prevails between l_1 and r_M / w_{1M}, l_2 and r_M / w_{2M}, respectively, if we take derivatives of both sides of the two equations, with respect to r_M / w_{1M} and r_M / w_{2M} separately:

$$(f_1 / f_1' - l_1)' = (\frac{f_1'^2 - f_1'' f_1}{f_1'^2} - 1) l_1' = -\frac{f_1'' f_1}{f_1'^2} l_1' = 1$$

$$(f_2 / f_2' - l_2)' = (\frac{f_2'^2 - f_2'' f_2}{f_2'^2} - 1) l_2' = -\frac{f_2'' f_2}{f_2'^2} l_2' = 1$$

with $l_1' = \frac{\partial l_1}{\partial \omega_1}$, $l_2' = \frac{\partial l_2}{\partial \omega_2}$, $\omega_1 = \frac{r_M}{w_{1M}}$ and $\omega_2 = \frac{r_M}{w_{2M}}$

For a given ratio of rental rate to wage rate, the labour intensity will be uniquely determined. Moreover, the prices can also be determined because they are functions of labour intensity. From equations (3ma), (5ma), and (1ma), we can put u_1 as a function of l_1 and thus also a function of ω_1.

$$u_1 = \frac{\varepsilon l_G}{f(l_1)} \quad \text{and} \quad u_2 = \frac{f(l_1) - \varepsilon l_G}{f(l_1)}.$$

From equation (4ma) we can determine the η_1 as:

$$\eta_1 = \frac{r_M - e}{u_2 f_2 P_2} \quad \text{and} \quad \eta_2 = \frac{u_2 f_2 P_2 - r_M + e}{u_2 f_2 P_2}.$$

From the equation of full employment we get:

$$l_2 + u_1(l_1 - l_2) = l_M$$

We differentiate both sides of the equation and obtain:

$$l_2' d\omega_2 = \frac{\varepsilon l_G}{f_1^2}(f_1(l_1' d\omega_1 - l_2' d\omega_2) - (l_1 - l_2) f_1' l_1' d\omega_1)$$

$$(1 - \frac{\varepsilon l_G}{f_1}) l_2' d\omega_2 + \frac{\varepsilon l_G}{f_1^2}(f_1 - (l_1 - l_2) f_1') l_1' d\omega_1 = 0, \tag{12ma}$$

Thus we get a relation between ω_1 and ω_2.

$$\frac{d\omega_1}{d\omega_2} = -\frac{(1 - \frac{\varepsilon l_G}{f_1}) l_2'}{\frac{\varepsilon l_G}{f_1^2}(f_1 - (l_1 - l_2) f_1') l_1'} < 0$$

Therefore, we can view ω_1 as a function of ω_2. Because ω_2 is a function of r_M, ω_1 is also a function of r_M, noting that w_{2M} is determined independently from r_M in (11ma). All the variables $l_1, l_2, u_1, u_2, \delta_1, \delta_2, P_{1M}, P_{2M}, w_{1M}$ can be uniquely determined, if r_M is given. We will use the minimum-wage condotion to determin the rental rate r_M. The minimum-wage condition is restated as follows:

$$u_2 f_2 P_{2M}(1 - \frac{f_2'(l_2)}{\delta_E}) = \frac{Y_{2P}}{K_M}(\frac{w_{2M}}{\delta_E} - P_{2P}). \tag{10m-b}$$

The right side of (10m-b) is a constant, while the left hand side is a function of r_M. We denote the left hand side as $D(r_M)$ and show that the derivative of $D(r_M)$ is positive.

$$d(D(r_M)) = (1 - \frac{f_2'(l_2)}{\delta_E})d(u_2 f_2 P_{2M}) + u_2 f_2 P_{2M} d(1 - \frac{f_2'(l_2)}{\delta_E}) \qquad (13\text{ma})$$

We begin by picking out the first part of the derivation and insert the equation (12ma) into it. Using the relation $f_2 P_{2M} = w_{2M} l_2 + r_M$, $du_1 = -du_2$ and $d\omega_2 = w_{2M} dr_M$ we get:

$$d(u_2 f_2 P_{2M}) = (w_{2M} l_2 + r_M) d(u_2) + u_2 d(w_{2M} l_2 + r_M)$$

$$= \frac{f_1' f_1 - f_1'(f_1 - \varepsilon l_G)}{f_1^2}(w_{2M} l_2 + r_M) l_1' d\omega_1 + \frac{f_1 - \varepsilon l_G}{f_1}(w_{2M} l_2' + w_{2M}) d\omega_2$$

$$= \frac{f_1' \varepsilon l_G}{f_1^2}(w_{2M} l_2 + r_M) l_1' d\omega_1 - w_{2M} \frac{\varepsilon l_G}{f_1}(1 - \frac{f_1'(l_1 - l_2)}{f_1}) l_1' d\omega_1 + u_2 w_{2M} d\omega_2$$

$$= \frac{w_{2M} \varepsilon l_G}{f_1}\left(\frac{f_1'(l_2 + \frac{r_M}{w_{2M}})}{f_1} - \frac{f_1 - f_1'(l_1 - l_2)}{f_1} \right) l_1' d\omega_1 + u_2 w_{2M} d\omega_2$$

$$= \frac{w_{2M} \varepsilon l_G}{f_1} 2\left(\frac{1}{f_1}\left(-f_1 + f_1'\left(l_2 + \frac{r_M}{w_{2M}} + l_1 - l_2 \right) \right) \right) l_1' d\omega_1 + u_2 w_{2M} d\omega_2$$

$$= \frac{w_{2M} \varepsilon l_G}{f_1} 2\left(\frac{1}{f_1}\left(-f_1 + f_1'\left(\frac{r_M}{w_{2M}} + l_1 \right) \right) \right) l_1' d\omega_1 + u_2 w_{2M} d\omega_2$$

$$= u_2 w_{2M} d\omega_2$$

Now we can place this result into the equation (13ma):

$$d(D(r_M)) = (1 - \frac{f_2'(l_2)}{\delta_E})(u_2 w_2 d\omega_2) - u_2 f_2 P_{2M} \frac{f_2''(l_2)}{\delta_E} l_2' d\omega_2$$

$$= (1 - \frac{f_2'(l_2)}{\delta_E})(u_2 w_2 d\omega_2) - u_2 f_2 P_{2M} \frac{f_2'^2(l_2)}{f_2(l_2) \delta_E} d\omega_2$$

$$= (1 - \frac{f_2'(l_2)}{\delta_E})(u_2 w_2 d\omega_2) - u_2 w_{2M} \frac{f_2'(l_2)}{\delta_E} d\omega_2$$

$$= u_2 w_2 d\omega_2$$

$$= u_2 dr_M$$

We obtain:

$$D(r_M)' = u_2 > 0$$

and

$$D(r_M)'' = u_2' = -u_1' = -\frac{\varepsilon l_G f_1'(l_1)}{f_1(l_1)^2} l_1' \cdot \frac{d\omega_1}{d\omega_2} \cdot \frac{d\omega_2}{dr_M} > 0.$$

As the first and second derivatives of $D(r_M)$ are all positive, $D(r_M)$ increases with rising r_M and $\lim_{r_M \to +\infty} D(r_M) = +\infty$. As r_M decreases to a certain point, it then holds then $f_2' = \delta_E$, or $D(r_M)=0$. Because $D(r_M)$ is a continuous and monotone increasing function, there must be a unique positive r_M^* for which the equation (10m-b) holds. That is to say that a unique equilibrium solution exists.

We can illustrate the equilibrium solution graphically in **Graph 4.1**. $D(r_M)$ is a rising function of r_M. For a given level of $d = \frac{Y_{2P}}{K_M}(\frac{w_{2M}}{\delta_E} - P_{2P})$, there is an r_M^*, so that $D(r_M^*)=d$.

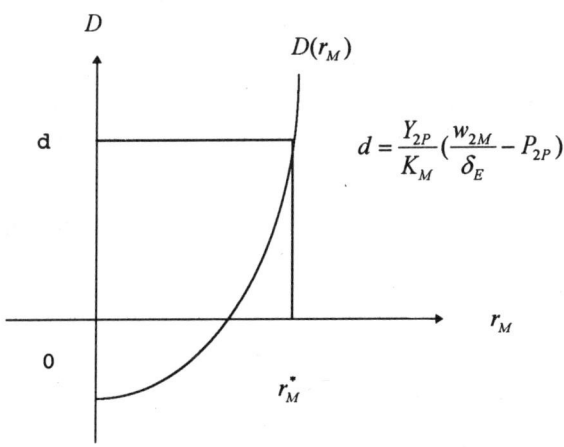

Graph 4.1 Existence of the Equilibrium

4.3 Stability of the Equilibrium

To examine the stability of the equilibrium we have to consider the reaction of the system to a disturbance away from equilibrium. We will adopt the idea of Walrasian tâtonnemont process. We specify the reactions of the prices to excess demand on the agricultural market and the industrial market, respectively.

The excess demand for agricultural products is the difference between demand and supply of these products.

$$E_{1M} = \varepsilon L_G - Y_{1M}$$

The total demand for industrial products is the total income minus the expenditure for agricultural products. (We assume the demand for food should be satisfied at first.) It can be expressed as follows:

$$w_P L_P + w_{2M} L_{2M} + w_{1M} L_{1M} + r_M K_M + r_P K_P - P_{1M} Y_{1M}$$
$$= w_P L_P + w_{2M} L_{2M} + r_P K_P + r_M K_{2M}$$
$$= P_{2M} Y_{2M} + P_{2P} Y_{2P}$$

The real demand for industrial products in the market segment can be written as the residual demand, because the price of the planned segment is lower than that of the market segment. Hence, the real demand for industrial products in the market segment must satisfy the following condition:

$$Y_{2M} = \frac{P_{2M} Y_{2M} + P_{2P} Y_{2P}}{\overline{P}_2} - Y_{2P}.$$

Then the real demand is:

$$Y_{2M}^d = \frac{Y_{2P}(\overline{P}_2 - P_{2P})}{(P_{2M} - \overline{P}_2)}$$

The excess demand can therefore be written as the difference between the real demand and the supply:

$$E_{2M} = Y_{2M}^d - Y_{2M}$$

We rewrite the excess demand in relation to capital stock of the market segment as follows.

$$e_{1M} = el_G - u_1 f_1$$

$$\text{with: } e_{1M} = \frac{E_{1M}}{K_M},$$

and

$$e_{2M} = \frac{k f_P(\overline{P} - P_{2P})}{(P_{2M} - \overline{P}_2)} - u_2 f_2$$

$$\text{with: } e_{2M} = \frac{E_{2M}}{K_M}, \ k = \frac{K_P}{K_M}, \ f_P = \frac{Y_P}{K_P}.$$

We assume an instantaneous adjustment process so that the short run dynamic process can be expressed as:

$$\frac{\partial P_{1M}}{\partial t} = h_1(e_{1M}) \quad \text{with } h_1(0) = 0 \quad \text{and} \quad h_1' > 0,$$

$$\frac{\partial P_{2M}}{\partial t} = h_2(e_{2M}) \quad \text{with } h_2(0) = 0 \quad \text{and} \quad h_2' > 0.$$

Without loss of generality, we assume $h_1'(0) = h_2'(0) = 1$. In the neighbourhood of an equilibrium, the following linear differential equation system holds:

$$\frac{\partial P_{1M}}{\partial t} = \frac{\partial e_{1M}}{\partial P_{1M}}(P_{1M} - P_{1M}^*) + \frac{\partial e_{1M}}{\partial P_{2M}}(P_{2M} - P_{2M}^*)$$

$$\frac{\partial P_{2M}}{\partial t} = \frac{\partial e_{2M}}{\partial P_{1M}}(P_{1M} - P_{1M}^*) + \frac{\partial e_{2M}}{\partial P_{2M}}(P_{2M} - P_{2M}^*)$$

The condition for a stabile solution of the system is:

$$\frac{\partial e_{1M}}{\partial P_{1M}} + \frac{\partial e_{2M}}{\partial P_{2M}} < 0$$

and

$$\frac{\partial e_{1M}}{\partial P_{1M}} \frac{\partial e_{2M}}{\partial P_{2M}} - \frac{\partial e_{1M}}{\partial P_{2M}} \frac{\partial e_{2M}}{\partial P_{1M}} > 0.$$

To check the stability, we calculate first the four partial derivatives for labour intensities. Rewriting equation (1ma) we get:

$$f_1 - f_1'(l_1)l_1 = \frac{r_M}{P_{1M}}.$$

Deriving both sides of the equation above with respect to P_{1M}, we get:

$$f_1'(l_1)\frac{\partial l_1}{\partial P_{1M}} - f_1'(l_1)\frac{\partial l_1}{\partial P_{1M}} - l_1 f_1''(l_1)\frac{\partial l_1}{\partial P_{1M}} = -\frac{r_M}{P_{1M}^2},$$

or

$$l_{11}' = \frac{\partial l_1}{\partial P_{1M}} = \frac{r_M}{l_1 f_1'(l_1) P_{1M}^2} < 0.$$

To calculate the partial derivatives with respect to P_{1M}, we treat P_{2M} as a constant. Considering equation (8ma), l_2 does not change with P_{1M}. We get:

$$l_{21}' = \frac{\partial l_2}{\partial P_{1M}} = 0.$$

From equation (8ma) we get:

$$l_{22}' = \frac{\partial l_2}{\partial P_{2M}} = \frac{-w_{2M}}{f_2''(l_2)P_{2M}^2} > 0.$$

From equation (2ma) we get:

$$f_2'(l_2)\frac{\partial l_2}{\partial P_{2M}} - f_2'(l_2)\frac{\partial l_2}{\partial P_{2M}} - l_2 f''(l_2)\frac{\partial l_2}{\partial P_{2M}} = -\frac{r_M' P_{2M} - r_{2M}}{P_{2M}^2},$$

thus:

$$r_M' = -P_{2M}^2 l_2 f''(l_2) l_{22}' + P_{2M} r_M > 0.$$

We multiply both sides of (1ma) by $f_1'(l_1)$ and derive it with respective to P_{2M}. We then get:

$$l_{12}' = \frac{\partial l_1}{\partial P_{2M}} = \frac{r_M'}{l_1 f_1''(l_1) P_{1M}} > 0.$$

Now we calculate the partial derivatives for the stability condition. Because the production function has a decreasing marginal productivity, $f_1 - f_1'(l_1)(l_1 - l_2)$ are always positive. We get:

$$\frac{\partial e_{1M}}{\partial P_{1M}} = -\frac{\partial(u_1 f_1)}{\partial P_{1M}} = -\frac{\partial}{\partial P_{1M}}\left(\frac{l_M - l_2}{l_1 - l_2} f_1(l_1)\right)$$

$$= \frac{-1}{(l_1 - l_2)^2}[f_1'(l_1)(l_M - l_2)(l_1 - l_2) l_{11}' - l_{11}'(l_M - l_2) f_1]$$

$$= \frac{l_{11}'}{(l_1 - l_2)^2}(l_M - l_2)(f_1 - f_1'(l_1)(l_1 - l_2)) < 0,$$

We use the relation: $l_1 > l_m > l_2$, because agricultural production is more labour intensive than industrial production.

$$\frac{\partial e_{2M}}{\partial P_{2M}} = -\frac{kf_P(\overline{P}_2 - P_{2P})}{(P_{2M} - \overline{P}_2)^2} - \frac{\partial(u_2 f_2)}{\partial P_{2M}} = -\frac{kf_P(\overline{P}_2 - P_{2P})}{(P_{2M} - \overline{P}_2)^2} - \frac{\partial}{\partial P_{2M}}\left(\frac{l_1 - l_M}{l_1 - l_2} f_2(l_2)\right)$$

$$= -\frac{kf_P(\overline{P}_2 - P_{2P})}{(P_{2M} - \overline{P}_2)^2} - \frac{1}{(l_1 - l_2)^2}[l_{12}' f_2(l_2)(l_M - l_2) + l_{22}'(l_1 - l_M)(f_2(l_2) + f_2'(l_2)(l_1 - l_2))] < 0,$$

$$\frac{\partial e_{1M}}{\partial P_{2M}} = -\frac{\partial(u_1 f_1)}{\partial P_{2M}} = -\frac{\partial}{\partial P_{2M}}\left(\frac{l_M - l_2}{l_1 - l_2} f_1(l_1)\right)$$

$$= \frac{1}{(l_1-l_2)^2}\left[l_{22}' f_1(l_2)(l_1-l_M) + l_{12}'(l_M-l_2)(f_1(l_1) - f_1'(l_1)(l_1-l_2))\right] > 0,$$

and

$$\frac{\partial e_{2M}}{\partial P_{1M}} = \frac{\partial}{\partial P_{1M}}\left(\frac{kf_P(\overline{P}_2 - P_{2P})}{(P_{2M} - \overline{P}_2)} - u_2 f_2\right) = -\frac{\partial(u_2 f_2)}{\partial P_{1M}} = \frac{\partial}{\partial P_{1M}}\left(\frac{l_1 - l_M}{l_1 - l_2} f_2(l_2)\right)$$

$$= \frac{-l_{11}'}{(l_1-l_2)^2}(l_M - l_2) f_2(l_2) > 0.$$

Obviously it holds that:

$$\frac{\partial e_{1M}}{\partial P_{1M}} + \frac{\partial e_{2M}}{\partial P_{2M}} < 0.$$

$$\frac{\partial e_{1M}}{\partial P_{1M}}\frac{\partial e_{2M}}{\partial P_{2M}} - \frac{\partial e_{1M}}{\partial P_{2M}}\frac{\partial e_{2M}}{\partial P_{1M}} = \frac{\partial e_{1M}}{\partial P_{1M}}\left(-\frac{kf_P(\overline{P}_2 - P_{2P})}{(P_{2M} - \overline{P}_2)^2}\right) + \frac{\partial u_1 f_1}{\partial P_{1M}}\frac{\partial u_2 f_2}{\partial P_{2M}} - \frac{\partial u_1 f_1}{\partial P_{2M}}\frac{\partial u_2 f_2}{\partial P_{1M}}$$

We insert the above results into the following expression and get:

$$\frac{\partial u_1 f_1}{\partial P_{1M}}\frac{\partial u_2 f_2}{\partial P_{2M}} - \frac{\partial u_1 f_1}{\partial P_{2M}}\frac{\partial u_2 f_2}{\partial P_{1M}}$$

$$= \frac{1}{(l_1-l_2)^4}\left[(-l_{11}' l_{22}')(l_1-l_2)^2(l_M-l_2)(f_1(l_1)f_2'(l_2) - f_1'(l_1)f_2(l_2) - f_1'(l_1)f_2'(l_2)(l_1-l_2))\right]$$

$$= \frac{1}{(l_1-l_2)^2}\left[(-l_{11}' l_{22}')(l_M-l_2)f_1'(l_1)f_2'(l_2)\left(\frac{f_1}{f_1'} - \frac{f_2}{f_2'} - (l_1-l_2)\right)\right]$$

$$= \frac{1}{(l_1-l_2)^2}\left[(-l_{11}' l_{22}')(l_M-l_2)f_1'(l_1)f_2'(l_2)\left(\frac{r_M}{w_{1M}} - \frac{r_M}{w_{2M}}\right)\right].$$

Under the assumption that the wage rate is lower in the agricultural sector than in the industrial sector, we get:

$$\frac{\partial u_1 f_1}{\partial P_{1M}}\frac{\partial u_2 f_2}{\partial P_{2M}} - \frac{\partial u_1 f_1}{\partial P_{2M}}\frac{\partial u_2 f_2}{\partial P_{1M}} > 0.$$

Therefore the stability condition is satisfied.

4.4 Long Run Dynamics

Long run dynamics is to be understood as the evolutionary path to a steady state, which consists of the equilibrium at each period during the transition process. Two cases may occur along a successful transition path. In the first one, the share of the market segment in the economy converges to one in the steady state. In the second case, the plan segment has to behave like the market segment during the transition process in order to survive within the system. These two cases may be interpreted as the completion of the transition from plan to market. Hence, in studying the long run dynamics of the system, both the transition path and the steady state are of interest. Each transition path will be examined under two aspects: whether there are constraining reasons such that the planned segment has to perform as the market segment to exist in the economy, and/or the share of the market segment in the economy will converge to one in the steady state. If neither case occurs during the transition process, the transition process from plan to market is not complete, i.e. there will be a coexistence of the planned segment and the market segment in the economy. We know that policies may influence the temporary equilibrium. Therefore, each evolutionary path should be examined under assumptions about chosen policies. Theoretically, there might be policies which only impact the evolutionary path but do not influence the steady state; or policies which affect both the path and the steady state. In Chapter 5 and 6, different policies will be analysed with respect to the transition path and the steady state. In this chapter, the long run dynamics are examined under the condition that no adjustment is made in the planned segment.

The long run dynamic property of the system is characterised by the dynamic equations of capital stock growth. The path of growth is the result of temporary equilibria. In a temporary equilibrium, the capital income is determined in both the planned segment and the market segment. The capital incomes determine, in turn, the investment in the two segments, respectively, and so the growth of the capital stocks in the two segments. As with the result of the different growth rates in the two segments, the ratio of the shortage of supply in the planned segment to the production capacity in the market segment will change. This ratio and capital stocks in both segments serve as a new initial condition for the next period. A new equilibrium is established according to this new initial condition.

The investment in the planned segment is determined as in the following equation:

$$\overline{P}_2 I_P^P(t) = r_P K_P$$

with: $I_P^P(t)$: the real investment in the planned segment
$\overline{P}_2$: average price of the industrial products.

The increment of the capital stock equals the net investment:

$$K_P(t) + K_P(t-1) = I_P^P(t) - \delta K_P(t)$$

The growth rate of the capital stock is:

$$\rho_P = \frac{K_P(t+1) - K_{1P}(t)}{K_P(t)}$$
$$= \frac{I^P(t) - \delta K(t)}{K_P(t)}$$
$$= \frac{r_P}{P_2} - \delta$$

Similarly, the following equation holds for the growth rate of the capital stock in the market segment:

$$\rho_M = \frac{r_M}{P_2} - \delta.$$

The ratio of the growth rate is expressed as follows:

$$\frac{\rho_P}{\rho_M} = \frac{r_P - \delta \overline{P_2}}{r_M - \delta \overline{P_2}}.$$

This equation simply says that different rental rates will lead to different growth rates of the capital stocks in the two segments and thus also different growth rates of the production. The rental rate can be determined as follows:

$$r_M = \frac{P_{2M} F_{2M} - w_{2M} L_{2M}}{K_{2M}} = P_{2M} \left(\frac{F_{2M}}{K_{2M}} - \frac{w_{2M}}{P_{2M}} \frac{L_{2M}}{K_{2M}} \right).$$

We define an H function as follows:

$$H(K, w/P) = \frac{F}{K} - \frac{w}{P} \frac{L(K, w/P)}{K}$$

The rental rate is the product of the Price P and the value of H-function:

$$r_M = P_{2M} H(K_M, w_{2M}/P_{2M}) \text{ and } r_P = P_{2P} H(K_P, w_P/P_{2P}).$$

It can be shown, that H is independent from K, if the production function is linearly homogenous:

$$\frac{\partial H}{\partial K} = \frac{1}{K^2}(K(F_K' + F_L'\frac{dL}{dK} + \frac{w}{P}\frac{dL}{dK}) - F + \frac{w}{P}L)$$

$$= \frac{1}{K^2}(KF_K' + F_L'L - F)$$

$$= 0$$

Therefore H depends only on the price and real wage rate. Furthermore, H is a decreasing function of the real wage rate:

$$\frac{\partial H}{\partial (w/P)} = \frac{1}{K}(F_L'\frac{dL}{d(w/P)} + \frac{w}{P}\frac{dL}{d(w/P)} - L(K, w/P)) = -L/K < 0$$

Because we have $P_{2P} < P_{2M}$ and $w_P > w_{2M}$, we obtain:

$$r_M = P_{2M}H(K_{2M}, w_{2M}/P_{2M}) > P_{2P}H(K_{2P}, w_P/P_{2P}) = r_{2P}$$

Hence, we conclude that the market segment will grow faster than the planned segment.

While the rental rate of capital in the planned segment is determined through chosen planning variables, the rental rate of capital in the market segment results from the temporary equilibrium. If the production technology and the demand structure of the economic subjects are given, the rental rate of capital in the market segment depends on the initial condition, especially on the initial ratio of capital stocks between the two segments. Thus, we can write the equations for the growth rates of capital stocks as follows:

$$\rho_P = r_P / \overline{P}_2 - \delta \quad \text{(A)}$$

$$\rho_M = r_M\left(\frac{K_P(t)}{K_M(t)}\right) / \overline{P}_2 - \delta \quad \text{(B)}$$

or

$$\rho_P = r_P / \overline{P}_2 - \delta \quad \text{(A-b)}$$

$$\rho_M(t) = r_M\left(\frac{K_P(0)\prod_{\tau=0}^{t-1}\rho_P(\tau)}{K_M(0)\prod_{\tau=0}^{t-1}\rho_M(\tau)}\right) / \overline{P}_2 - \delta. \quad \text{(B-b)}$$

If the exogenous variables remain unchanged, it holds that $r_M > r_P$ and $\lim_{t \to \infty} r_M \neq \lim_{t \to \infty} r_P$. Then $\lim_{t \to \infty} \rho_M \neq \lim_{t \to \infty} \rho$ follow. Thus, the ratio of capital stocks converges to zero. The dynamic system (A-B) converges to a stationary point, where the following equations hold:

$$\lim_{t \to \infty} r_M = r_M \left(\lim_{t \to \infty} \frac{K_P(0) \prod_{\tau=0}^{t-1} \rho_P(\tau)}{K_M(0) \prod_{\tau=0}^{t-1} \rho_M(\tau)} \right) = r_M(0) = r_M^*,$$

and

$$\lim_{t \to \infty} \rho_P = \rho_P = r_P / \overline{P}_2 - \delta,$$

$$\lim_{t \to \infty} \rho_M = r_M^* / \overline{P}_2 - \delta.$$

Because the ratio of the capital stock of the planned segment to that of the market segment converges to zero in the steady state, the right hand side of (10ma) will be zero. The stationary rental rate can be determined from the minimum wage condition:

$$u_2 f_2 (P_{2M} - \frac{w_{2M}}{\delta_E}) = 0$$

or

$$P_{2M}(r_M^*) = \frac{w_{2M}}{\delta_E}$$

Also, $f_2'(l_2^*) = \delta_E$ and $r_M^* = w_{2M}(f_2 / f_2' - l_2^*)$

The economic implication of this long run steady state is that at the end of the transition process the market segment is the dominant part of the system. The share of the market segment converges to 1. Economic activities, such as the pricing of factors and products, allocation of resources, are co-ordinated through the market mechanism. The share of the planned segment converges to zero. The planned segment no longer plays any significant role in the economy.

The dynamic process described above is only valid for the case with $r_M^* \geq e$. If the inequity does not hold, r_M^* will be smaller then e. $r_M^* < e$ implies that the disequilibrium of the planned segment is too big to be corrected by a relative small market segment. The production of consumer goods in the market segment can not compensate for the shortage of supply in the planned segment, even if all the productive capacities in the market segment are used to produce the consumer goods. Hence, the production of the market segment is restricted in the consumer sector. The market segment can only reduce the problem of the economy to some extent but not remove it totally. The shortage of supply still persists. The whole economy is in a state of disequilibrium. This is especially true at the beginning of the economic reform, when the productive capacity of the market segment is very small.

It is of great interest to ask whether this state can change over into a state of equilibrium during the evolutionary process, or whether it is possible for the market segment to expand into the investment sector? To answer this question, we will examine the growth process in the case with $r_M < e$. In this case, it is necessary to replace equation (3mb) and (4mb) through $\eta_2 = 1$ and $\eta_1 = 0$. Because there is still an unsatisfied demand for consumption, the forced saving is not to be avoided. The growth process in the planned segment, which is described in the equation (A), should be modified. The investment in the planned segment is equal to the sum of the capital income and the forced savings. The equation for the growth rate of the capital stock in the planned segment can be modified as in the following equation:

$$\rho_P = \frac{r_P + \rho E / K_P}{\overline{P}_2} - \delta \quad \text{with:} \quad \rho = \frac{e}{r_M^*} - 1 \quad . \quad \text{(Ac)}$$

where ρE is the amount of the forced savings. ρ is between 1 and 0, and is the fraction of the forced saving in total unsatisfied demand. $\rho = 1$ means that the market segment does not cover any demand for consumption in the planned segment so that forced savings are equal to the total unsatisfied demand.

The equation for the capital growth rate in the market segment remains unchanged. Now it holds that $r_M K_M = (1-\rho)E$. We insert this in equation (Ac):

$$\rho_P = \frac{r_P + (E - r_M K_M)/K_P}{\overline{P}_2} - \delta$$

$$= \frac{r_P + h \cdot (1 - r_M / e)}{\overline{P}_2} - \delta$$

$$\text{with } h = \frac{E}{K_P}$$

The dynamic process of the system is now given through the following two equations:

$$\rho_P = \frac{r_P + h \cdot (1 - r_M / e)}{\overline{P}_2} - \delta$$

$$\rho_M = r_M / \overline{P}_2 - \delta$$

The dynamic property of the system depends on whether r_M is larger or smaller than $r_P + h \cdot (1 - r_M/e)$ and how the difference between them changes in the evolutionary process. At first we look at the changing rate of the difference by deriving the difference respective to r_M.

$$(r_P + h(1 - r_M/e) - r_M)' = h \frac{-e + r_M e' - e^2/h}{e^2} = h \frac{r_M e' - e(1 + e/h)}{e^2}$$

Considering the equation (10ma)) we obtain:

$$e = \frac{E}{K_M} = \frac{bY_P}{K_M} \frac{b}{\overline{P}_2 - P_{2P}} = \frac{Y_P}{K_M}(\overline{P}_2 - P_{2P}) = \frac{b}{\overline{P}_2 - P_{2P}} D(r_M),$$

and

$$e' = \frac{b}{\overline{P}_2 - P_{2P}} D'(r_M) = \frac{bu_2}{\overline{P}_2 - P_{2P}} > 0.$$

$$r_M e' - e(1 + e/h) = \frac{b}{\overline{P}_2 - P_{2P}}(r_M u_2 - (1 + \frac{e}{h})u_2 f_2(P_{2M} - \overline{P}_2))$$

$$= \frac{bu_2}{\overline{P}_2 - P_{2P}}(r_M - (1 + \frac{K_P}{K_M}) f_2(P_{2M} - \overline{P}_2))$$

$$= -\frac{bu_2}{\overline{P}_2 - P_{2P}}(f_2(\frac{K_P}{K_M}(P_{2M} - \overline{P}_2) - \overline{P}_2) + w_{2M} l_2)$$

$$= -\frac{bu_2}{\overline{P}_2 - P_{2P}}(f_2(\frac{K_P}{K_M} P_{2M} - (1 + \frac{K_P}{K_M})\overline{P}_2) + w_{2M} l_2)$$

For $K_M \ll K_P$ and $P_{2M} \gg P_{2P}$ we obviously obtain $(r_P + h(1 - r_M/e) - r_M)' < 0$. That is if the capital stock in the planned segment is much larger than that in the market segment, the difference between the growth rates in the two segments decreases.

If $r_M < r_P + h \cdot (1 - r_M/e)$ is true, the planned segment will grow faster. The disequilibrium indicator $e = \frac{E}{K_M} = \frac{hK_P}{K_M}$ and the rental rate in the market segment will increase until the difference between r_M and $r_P + h \cdot (1 - r_M/e)$ vanishes[57]. Then the system will grow at a constant rate. Both the planned and the market segments will take a constant share in the system. Therefore, at a certain time the rates of growth in both segments will be equal, as long as the rental rate of capital does not exceed the critical point e first[58]. From this point on, the two segments

---

[57] If the difference does not vanish, the planned segment will grow all the time faster than the market segment. The share of market segment will converge to zero.
[58] This case can only occur, when the economy is intervened by policy.

will grow at the same rate and $\frac{E}{K_M}$ will remain constant. Each segment will take a constant share in the economy, i.e. the planned segment and the market segment exist parallel in the long run. But the share of the market segment is very small, because the growth rate of the planned segment has always been larger than that of the market segment.

The economic implication of this case is rather direct. The restriction of the production to the consumer sector implies, on the one hand, that the shortage situation in the economy is only quantitatively reduced but not totally removed so that the main characteristic of CPE remains. On the other hand, the forced saving is used to support the quantity drive in the planned segment so that the shortage is continuously reproduced. In this case, the market segment only plays a complementary role in the economy. It reduces the shortage to some extent, but remains dependent on the planned segment. Furthermore, the share of the market segment is smaller than the initial share and the planned economic activities are the dominant part of the economy. The typical phenomena of CPE such as shortage of supply, inflexible production structure and fix prices will not diminish. The market segment reduces problems in the planned economy only to certain degree. The transition process will not proceed successfully.

In most more realistic cases, it holds that $r_M > r_P + h \cdot (1 - r_M/e)$. We can demonstrate this result through the following calculation supposing that μ is the ratio of the shortage to the total consumption expenditure. It may be a real number between zero and 30%.[59] α is the fraction of labour income to total income. For the production of industrial goods α may be less than 60%. We then calculate $h = \frac{E}{K_P} = \frac{\mu w_P L_P}{K_P} = \mu \frac{\alpha}{1-\alpha} r_P$. Hence, h is much smaller than the rental rate in the planned segment. The rental rate in the market segment is much larger than the rental rate in the planned segment, because the market prices are much higher than the planned prices, especially when the production capacity in the market segment is still very small. Hence, it is more realistic that $r_M^* > r_P + h \cdot (1 - r_M^*/e)$, noting that r_M^* is assumed to be smaller than e. In this case the market segment will grow quickly. $r_M^* > r_P + h \cdot (1 - r_M^*/e)$ and $(r_P + h \cdot (1 - r_M^*/e) - r_M^*)' < 0$ imply that the market segment will grow faster until the production of the market segment expands over both sectors of the economy. The transition process will continue.

---

[59] We take 30% as an over estimation of the disequilibrium situation.

Chapter 5

Analysis of the Driving Forces of the Transition

The transition process in the model is based on the difference in growth between the two segments. The driving forces of the transition are those that can influence the growth in both the market segment and the planned segment. Three kinds of causes can lead to the difference in growth of both segments. First, the growth mechanism is different in the two segments. Because the economic activities in the two segments function according to distinct principles, the growth mechanisms work differently. This difference is the most important force for the transition from plan to market. The changing behaviour in the planned segment constitutes the second kind of cause. The change in the planned segment is, in part, an adjustment to the new situation in the economy, forced by competition from the market segment. The change is partially the result of economic reform policies. The last kind of cause consists of the interactions in the form of transaction and competition between the two segments. The transaction is realised by material flows and financial flows between the two segments. These flows are key to the dynamic property of the system. Various policies can influence the flows between the two segments and thus the transition process.

In the following section we will analyse these three causes and examine their impact on the transition process.

5.1 The Planned Segment and Kalecki's Model

In our model, the growth mechanism of the planned segment has the pattern of growth in Kalecki's Model. We assume that the price and the wage rate in the planned segment are given exogenously. From the linearly homogenous production we find that the cost minimising labour demand depends linearly on the capital stock.

$$L_P = \alpha\left(\frac{w_P}{P_P}\right)K_P$$

Thus, the production also depends linearly on the capital stock.

$$Y_P = F(K_P, \alpha\left(\frac{w_P}{P_P}\right)K_P) = F(1, \alpha\left(\frac{w_P}{P_P}\right))K_P = \phi\left(\frac{w_P}{P_P}\right)K_P$$

The increment of production results from the increment of the capital stock.

$$\Delta Y_P = \phi\left(\frac{w_P}{P_P}\right)\Delta K_P = \phi\left(\frac{w_P}{P_P}\right)(I - \delta K_P) = \phi\left(\frac{w_P}{P_P}\right)I - \delta Y_P$$

The growth rate of production is:

$$g = \frac{\Delta Y_P}{Y_P} = \phi i - \delta \quad \text{or} \quad g + \phi c = \phi - \delta$$

with: $i = \frac{I}{Y}$ share of productive accumulation,

$c = \frac{C}{Y}$ share of consumption.

If we compare this equation with the fundamental equation in Kalecki's model (see section 2.1.3.), we see that the equation in our model is a special case with a production function of constant returns to scale.

As $\phi - \delta$ is independent from the decision, the decision about the growth is a „trade off" between the growth rate and the contemporary consumption. This is exactly the growth pattern described by Kalecki. Because wage income is the main source of consumption, the political desire for quick growth is instrumentalised by keeping the wage rate at a low level. The evidence for the pursuit of this policy is the fact that in China, despite a rather considerable growth rate of the GNP during the sixties and seventies, there was no remarkable improvement of the living standard. In fact, the real average wage in 1983 did not reach the level of that in 1957[60]. Nevertheless, even this low level of consumption could not be satisfied because in the practice of CPE the production of consumer goods often had to give way to the production of investment goods.

Table 5.1 Index of real wage and the annual growth rate of national income

Year	Growth rate of national income (%)	Index of average real wage
1952	14(1953)	100
1957	4.5	127.9
1962	-6.5	92.1
1965	17	110.1
1970	23	105.6

---

[60] See Chinese Statistic Year book 1988 p.190 Tab.4-35.

1975	8.3	107.9
1980	6.4	124.7
1981	4.9	123.4
1982	8.3	124.9
1983	9.8	126.7
1984	13.5	145.6

Source: Chinese Statistic Year Book 1988 p.52 and p.190.

During the economic reform, this kind of growth pattern changed significantly. First, the source of growth came not only from investment in the planned segment, but also from investment in the market segment. The supply deficit of consumer goods in the planned segment was met by the transaction between the planned segment and the market segment. At same time, the investment goods produced in the planned segment were bought by the market segment to enlarge the production capacity there. The rate of growth was the result of the equilibrium state determined by the market forces. The CPE specific logic of the growth mechanism, „the trade-off between growth and contemporary consumption", does not function here any longer. Growth is no more a simple matter of a decision by the planning authority.

5.2 The Market Segment and the Dualistic Economic Model

The dualistic features of the model are expressed through the asymmetric treatment of the two sectors in the market segment. According to Kelley, „the existence of dualism has been argued on the basis of difference in (1) social system, (2) racial or ethnic background, (3) production condition, (4) demographic behaviour, (5) consumer expenditure and consumer savings behaviour, and (6) the domestic and foreign sectors."[61] In our model the dualism lies, primarily, in the differential production condition. The production in the agricultural sector is assumed to be always more labour intensive than in the industrial sector. Secondly, the agricultural sector is expected to absorb all labour forces which can not be utilised in the industrial sector. Although the wage rate in the industrial sector is postulated at a level of existence minimum in the urban areas, the wage rate in the agricultural sector lies even lower, which implies that the living standard is different in the rural and urban areas. Thirdly, we have assumed an asymmetric consumer expenditure in two sectors. (For simplicity, the demand for agricultural product was assumed to be inelastic.)

---

[61] See:Kelley, Williamson, and Cheetham (1972) p.8-9.

If we neglect the planned segment, the model would become a dualistic model with a two sectors neo-classic general equilibrium framework. (The model could also be viewed as a special case of the dualistic model developed by Kelley Williamson and Cheetham[62].) The growth in the market segment leads to structural change in the economy, due to the dualistic properties of the two sectors in the economy. This structural change may be understood as the process of industrialisation, where the share of industrial production is increasing and the labour force continuously moves from agriculture into industry. Now the question is naturally raised: why did the industrialisation process not take place earlier? In the following section, we will explain why this industrialisation process did not take place until the beginning of the economic reform.

5.3 The Rural Reform and Stimulation of Transition

The Chinese agriculture feeds more than 1 billion people and provides jobs for more than 80% of the population. Before the economic reform, agriculture in China was integrated into the planning system through an obligated quantity planning and a strict price control. Moreover, peasants were only allowed to engage in agricultural production. Any activities in other sectors were strictly controlled through the bureaucratic administration. The farmers had to fulfil the planned target of production. They had to deliver to the state a given amount of products required by the urban population, and they also had to produce enough food for themselves. In this case, the decision of farmers could be modelled as follows:

$$\frac{\partial F_{1M}}{\partial L_{1M}} = \frac{w_1^\circ}{P_{1P}}$$ with: P_{1P} the planned price for agricultural product

w_1° the prevailing wage rate

The amount of capital stock is irrelevant because farmers could only use their capital for agriculture. Before the reform, they had to carry out the production plan of the state, even if it was economically unprofitable. We assume that the planned amount was higher than the optimal amount such that the agricultural production was unprofitably run. The surplus labour force was another burden for agriculture. We can demonstrate the situation of agriculture in the graph below (see **Graph 5.1**):

---

[62] See: Kelley, Williamson, and Cheetham (1972).

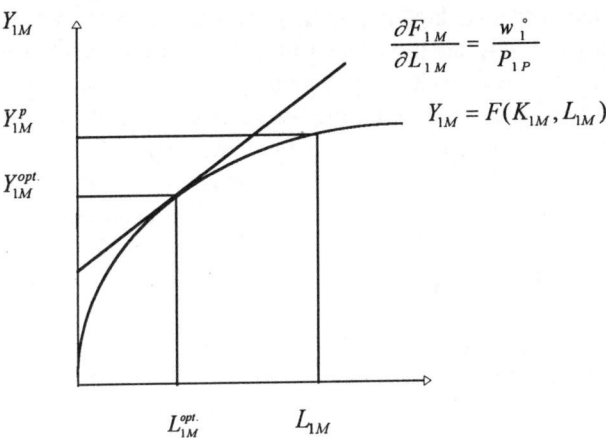

Graph 5.1. Influence of planning on agriculture

The optimal decision for the farmer would be $L_{1M}^{opt.}$ with a production amount $Y_{1M}^{opt.}$ lower than the planned production Y_{1M}^{p}. Because the planned target was obligatory, everything was done to fulfil the plan. This means more labour input was used, even if the marginal productivity was lower than the real wage rate, which is supposed to have reached its lower limit. Another reason for the unprofitable usage of labour in the agriculture was that agriculture had to absorb all the surplus labour which could not be utilised in the industrial sector.[63] This economic loss through the usage of surplus labour resulted in a reduction of the capital income. Thus, the following equation holds:

$$\frac{\partial F_{1M}}{\partial K_{1M}} > \frac{r_1}{P_{1P}}$$

and

$$\frac{\partial F_{1M}}{\partial L_{1M}} < \frac{w_1^\circ}{P_{1P}}.$$

The capital income can be determined residually through the difference between total income and the labour income.

$$r_1 = \frac{P_{1P} Y_{1M} - w_1^\circ L_{1M}}{K_{1M}}$$

---

[63] For detail discussion see also: Perish (1990) and Perkins (1990).

If the price is so low that the rental rate of capital can only keep pace with the depreciation, the marginal labour productivity will not rise. Consequently, the labour productivity, and thus the standard of living of farmers can not decisively improve. The agricultural production available for the state can not rise either, i.e. there is no chance for agriculture to improve. Before the reform, the low planned price of agricultural products and the bureaucratically controlled production manner had been the main obstacles to development in the rural area. It destroyed the economic vitality of agriculture so that a spontaneous industrialisation became economically impossible.

In the following **Table 5.2** we can see that from the beginning of the sixties to the beginning of the economic reform (in 1978), the planned price did not change significantly.

Table 5.2 Planned price index for agricultural products

Year	Planned price index
1952	121,6
1957	146,2
1962	200,1
1965	187,9
1970	195,1
1975	208,7
1978	217,4
1980	284,4
1985	362,9
1990	595,8
1991	583,9
1992	603,8
1993	684,7
1994	844,9

Source: Chinese Statistic Year Book 1993 p.238
          Chinese Statistic Year Book 1995 p.233

The rising price of agricultural products, as practised at the beginning of the rural reform and the decollectivization, has given a big push in the development of agriculture.

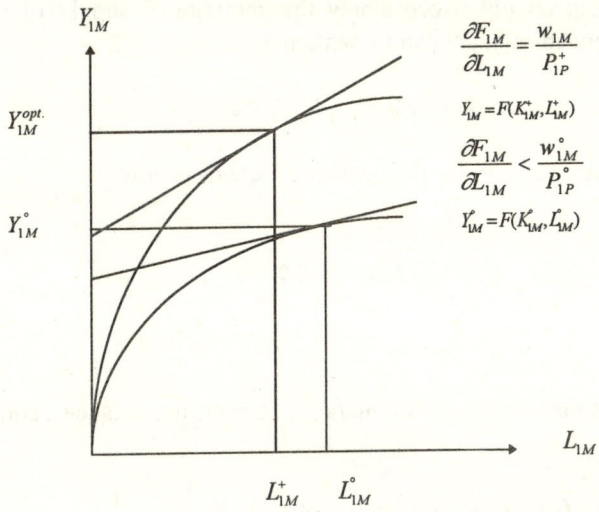

Graph 5.2. Impact of rural reform on agriculture

There are two direct effects as a result of rising prices. First, rising prices lead to increases in the rental rate of capital. Farmers are able to put more capital into production, which in turn leads to increases in labour productivity. The production curve turns upwards (see **Graph 5.2**). Secondly, the real wage rate in terms of agricultural price decreases; it is thus more profitable to use labour force than before the reform. These two effects result in increasing production. If the increase in production is big enough so that the supply of agricultural products at the old level of the labour input is larger than the food demand, the level of employment in agriculture decreases. Marginal productivity rises in agriculture. Improvement of the farmers' living standard is economically founded. From then on the expansion of the capital stock in the rural area and the labourers freed from agriculture transfer into industrial production. (We assume in the model, that since the beginning of the economic reform the price of agricultural products was set so high that the optimal production of the farmers exceeds the planned production, and can thus satisfy the demand for agricultural products.)

5.4 Savings and Financial Market

In the previous discussion we assumed that the wage saving fraction is zero and that of capital income is 100%. A more realistic assumption would be

$0 \leq s_{wM} \leq s_r \leq 1$ and $0 \leq s_{wP} \leq s_r \leq 1$, where s_{wM}, s_{wP}, s_r are the saving fractions of labour income in the market segment, the plan segment and the saving fraction of capital income, respectively. Accordingly the shortage of supply of consumer products in the planned segment can be written as:

$$E = (1-s_{wP})w_P L_P + (1-s_r)r_P K_P - P_{2P}C_{2P} > 0$$

The market balance condition for the investment goods is now:

$$P_{2M}I_{2M} + P_{2P}I_{2P}$$
$$= s_r r_M K_M + s_{wM}(L_{1M}W_{1M} + L_{2M}W_{2M}) + s_{wP}L_P w_P + s_r r_P K_P$$

or $\qquad P_{2M}I_{2M} = s_r r_M K_M + s_{wM}(L_{2M}W_{2M} + L_{1M}W_{1M}) - E$.

In relation to the capital stock of the market segment, the balance condition can be written as:

$$\eta_1 u_2 P_{2M} f_2 = s_r r_M + s_{wM}(u_2 l_2 w_{2M} - u_1 l_1 w_{1M}) - e.$$

Now the basic model in chapter 4 can be modified as follows, to account for different saving behaviours:

$$f_1/f_1' - l_1 = \frac{r_M}{w_{2M}} \qquad (1\text{mb})$$

$$f_2/f_2' - l_2 = \frac{r_M}{w_{2M}} \qquad (2\text{mb})$$

$$u_1 f_1 = \varepsilon l_G \qquad (3\text{mb})$$

$$u_1 + u_2 = 1 \qquad (4\text{mb})$$

$$\eta_1 u_2 P_{2M} f_2 = s_r r_M + s_{wM}(u_2 l_2 w_{2M} - u_1 l_1 w_{1M}) - e \qquad (5\text{mb})$$

$$\eta_1 + \eta_2 = 1 \qquad (6\text{mb})$$

$$P_{1M} = \frac{w_{2M}}{f_1'} \qquad (7\text{mb})$$

$$P_{2M} = \frac{w_{2M}}{f_2'} \qquad (8\text{ma})$$

$$l_1 u_1 + l_2 u_2 = l_M \qquad \text{(9mb)}$$

$$u_2 f_2 (P_{2M} - \overline{P}_2) = \frac{Y_{2P}}{K_M}(P_{2P} - \overline{P}_2) \qquad \text{(10mb)}$$

If we compare this modified system with different saving fractions to the basic model described in chapter 4, we find, that the saving behaviour only influences the distribution of production between consumer goods and investment goods within the industrial sector. The argument for the existence, uniqueness and stability of equilibrium also holds in this case as in chapter 4.

However, with different saving behaviours the dynamics of capital accumulation should be modified accordingly. We assume that all savings from labour income will be used for investment through the banking system, which is still under rather strong central control. It is essential how the savings from labour income are distributed between the two segments. We suppose that the savings of capital income will be invested in the same segment. We denote κ as the share of savings from labour income, which is used for investment in the plan segment. The capital stock accumulation in the two segments can be described through the following two equations. We denote the sum of savings from the labour income with $S = s_{wM}(L_{1M}w_{1M} + L_{2M}w_{2M}) + s_{wP}L_P w_P$.

$$\rho_P = 1 - \delta + (s_r r_P + \kappa \frac{S}{K_P(t)})/\overline{P}_2 \qquad \text{(Ab)}$$

$$\rho_M = 1 - \delta + (s_r r_M + (1-\kappa)\frac{S}{K_P(t)})/\overline{P}_2 \qquad \text{(Bb)}$$

Similar to the case of the basic model, the difference between $s_r r_P + \kappa S / K_P$ and $s_r r_M + (1-\kappa)S / K_M$ is key to the dynamic behaviour of the system. The difference depends first of all on the rental rate in both segments. It also depends on the distribution of saved labour income. As discussed above, the rental rate in the market segment is higher than that in the planned segment. If the difference between the rental rates outweighs the saving fraction (i.e. if it holds that $s_r r_P + \kappa S / K_P < s_r r_M$), the market segment will always have a faster growth rate. The share of the planned segment in the economy will diminish. Of course, this assumption can only hold if the saving fraction of labour income is very small. Generally, we may have to consider the case in which the inequality does not hold. In this case, the long run behaviour of the system depends on the distribution of the labour income saved. If there is no competitive financial market, which is exactly the case in China, the flow of financial asset will run according to administrative rules. The simplest rule is that distribution is held at a fixed ratio. κ is supposed to be constant between 0 and 1. For a given κ, even if $s_r r_M + (1-\kappa)S / K_M$ is larger than $s_r r_P + \kappa S / K_P$, the share of the planned segment will not diminish, because the former will decrease faster than the latter until they are equal. Then the planned segment will take a constant share in the economy. In case the former is smaller than the latter, the planned segment will grow faster. However, the difference between them will converge to zero so that in the long run the growth rates in both segments will be equal.

If the saving of labour income is distributed somehow competitively, the enterprises in the market segment have a better chance to get financial asset than those in the planned segment. They can pay a higher interest rate because the rental rate in the market segment is higher. Supposing that the savings are distributed in proportion to the capital stock in both segments, κ could be calculated as follows :

$$\kappa = \frac{K_P}{K_P + K_M}.$$

The growth rates of the capital stock in both segments are:

$$\rho_P = 1 - \delta + (s_r r_P + \frac{K_P}{K_P + K_M} S/K_P)/\overline{P}_2 = 1 - \delta + (s_r r_P + \frac{S}{K_P + K_M})/\overline{P}_2 \qquad (Ab^*)$$

$$\rho_M = 1 - \delta + (s_r r_M + \frac{K_M}{K_P + K_M} \frac{S}{K_M})/\overline{P}_2 = 1 - \delta + (s_r r_M + \frac{S}{K_P + K_M})/\overline{P}_2 \qquad (Bb^*)$$

Obviously, the growth rate in the market segment will be higher than in the planned segment, and thus the share of the plan segment in the economy will diminish. In other words, the transition from plan to market will proceed.

The discussion above has shown that the reform of the financial market is crucial for the transition from plan to market. The transition process will be impeded if the financial market is run administratively and the financial flow does not react to the situation on the market. The financial market will become even more important if the allocation of the capital income is also deposited on the financial market.

5.5 Tax Policy

Tax policy is one of the most important instruments for the government to intervene in the economy, especially in the market segment. In this section we will analyse the influence of tax policy on the transition process. Because the transition from plan to market is understood as the increase/decrease in the share of the market segment/(planned segment), we only have to examine the impact of tax policy on the growth of the capital stock in the two segments. It is important to distinguish between tax spent for consumption and for investment because these two kinds of uses have a different impact on the growth of the capital stock.

Tax Used for Consumption:

We assume that a constant tax rate is charged on the capital income[64]. This policy leads to a larger share in capital income being used for consumption. For simplicity, we assume $s_{wM} = s_{wP} = 0$. The deficit of supply for consumption products in the planned segment is expressed in the following equation:

$$E^° = w_P L_P + t_r r_P K_P + (1-s_r)(1-t_r)r_P K_P - P_{2P} C_{2P}$$

The market balance for the investment good is expressed as:

$$P_{2M} I_{2M} = s_r(1-t_r)r_M K_M - E^°$$

and for consumer goods:

$$P_{2M} C_{2M} = (1-s_r)(1-t_r)r_M K_M + w_{1M} L_{1M} + w_{2M} L_{2M} + t_r r_M K_M + E^°$$

The sub-model for the market segment now consists of the following 10 equations:

$$f_1/f_1' - l_1 = \frac{r_M}{w_{2M}} \qquad (1mc)$$

$$f_2/f_2' - l_2 = \frac{r_M}{w_{2M}} \qquad (2mc)$$

$$u_1 f_1 = \varepsilon l_G \qquad (3mc)$$

$$u_1 + u_2 = 1 \qquad (4mc)$$

$$\eta_1 u_2 P_{2M} f_2 = s_r(1-t_r)r_M - e^° \qquad (5mc)$$

$$\eta_1 + \eta_2 = 1 \qquad (6mc)$$

$$P_{1M} = \frac{w_{2M}}{f_1'} \qquad (7mc)$$

---

[64] The tax on wage is neglected, because the income of most wage-erners is well below the taxation limit.

$$P_{2M} = \frac{w_{2M}}{f_2'} \qquad (8mc)$$

$$l_1 u_1 + l_2 u_2 = l_M \qquad (9mc)$$

$$u_2 f_2 (P_{2M} - \overline{P}_2) = \frac{Y_{2P}}{K_M}(P_{2P} - \overline{P}_2) \qquad (10mc)$$

Obviously the argument for the existence, uniqueness, and stability of the equilibrium solution holds here as in the case of the basic model in chapter 4. The difference is that the expenditure of tax income for consumption raises the final demand for consumption so that the portion of consumer goods in the whole industrial production increases. The growth of capital stocks in the two segments can be determined accordingly:

$$\rho_P = s_r(1-t_r)r_P / \overline{P}_2 - \delta \qquad (Ac)$$

$$\rho_P = s_r(1-t_r)r_M / \overline{P}_2 - \delta \qquad (Bc)$$

These two equations differ from the equations (A) and (B) in chapter 4 only in the positive factor $s_r(1-t_r)$. Hence, the conclusion about the long run dynamic property of the system also holds in this case. The imposed tax only slows down the growth of the capital stocks in both segment. But the growth is faster in the market segment than in the planned segment so that in the long run the share of planned segment will converge to zero. In other words, the transition proceeds.

Tax used for investment in the planned segment:

If the tax income is completely used for investment in the planned segment, the growth rate in the planned segment will naturally benefit. We will examine the impact of this policy on the transition process. The deficit of supply for consumption in the planned segment is written as:

$$E = w_P L_P + (1-t_r)(1-s_r)r_P K_P - P_{2P} C_{2P}$$

The market balance condition for investment goods in the market segment can be written as follows:

$$P_{2M} I_{2M} = s_r(1-t_r)r_M K_M - E + t_r r_M K_M$$

For consumption products:

$$P_{2M}C_{2M} = (1-s_r)(1-t_r)r_M K_M + w_{1M}L_{1M} + w_{2M}L_{2M} + E - P_{1M}Y_{1M}$$

In the equation system from (1mc) to (10mc) only one of the equations, (5mc), has to be modified to account for larger demand for investment products.

$$\eta_2 u_2 P_{2M} f_2 = (s_r(1-t_r)+t_r)r_M - e \qquad (5\text{mc-b})$$

Similar to the case of using tax income merely for consumption, the equilibrium solution is unique. However, the long run property of the system changes. Instead of the diminishing share of the planned segment in the economy, the planned segment takes at least a constant share over time. The growth rates of the capital stock in the two segments are, respectively:

$$\rho_P = (s_r(1-t_r)r_P + \frac{t_r r_M K_M + t_r r_P K_P}{K_P})/\overline{P_2} - \delta$$

$$= (s_r(1-t_r)+t_r)r_P + \frac{t_r r_M K_M}{K_P})/\overline{P_2} - \delta \qquad (\text{Ac-b})$$

$$\rho_M = s_r(1-t_r)r_M / \overline{P_2} - \delta \qquad (\text{Bc-b})$$

The difference between $(s_r(1-t_r)+t_r)r_P + \frac{t_r r_M K_M}{K_P}$ and $s_r(1-t_r)r_M$ is decisive for the long run behaviour of the system. It is worthy of note, $(s_r(1-t_r)+t_r)r_P + \frac{t_r r_M K_M}{K_P}$ increases, as $s_r(1-t_r)r_M$ decreases, as long as $s_r(1-t_r)r_M > (s_r(1-t_r)+t_r)r_P + \frac{t_r r_M K_M}{K_P}$ holds. With the progress of the evolution, the difference between the growth rates in the two segments becomes increasingly smaller until they are equal. Both segments will then take a constant share in the economy and the transition will cease.

The tax income may also be used for investment in the market segments, through subsidies or supports for the enterprises of the market segment. For the long run dynamic property of the system, it becomes crucial how total investment which is financed through the tax income, is distributed between the two segments. Similar to the discussion in the section 5.4, we may conclude that if the total investment fond is distributed with a constant fraction for each segment, both segments will have a constant share in the economy in the long run. The transition will not be carried out to the end. If the total investment fund is distributed in proportion to the production capacities of the two segments, the share of planned segment will converge to zero. The transition will proceed to the end.

5.6 Adjustment of the Planned Segment

With the appearance of the market segment, the economic environment changes in the economy. There are two prices for the same product. The first one is the planned price, which is determined and controlled by the planning authority. The second one is the market price, which results from demand and supply on the market and always lies above the planned price. The higher price in the market segment results in the higher rental rate of capital in the market segment, which leads in turn to the faster growth in the market segment. The flourish of the market segment motivates the planned segment to adjust itself to the new situation. During the economic reform, where the profitability and efficiency of a enterprises is always the central topic of management, managers become conscious of price as an instrument of management. In the following section we will discuss a few variations of the price adjustment in the planned segment.

5.6.1 Partial Price Adjustment

With partial price adjustment we denote a certain kind of price policy during the reform, where the planned price for industrial goods is raised to reduce its difference to the market price. Because price raising implies at same time the radical decrease of the real wage, which would reduce the living standard of workers and cause social disturbance, the planning authority tends to raise the wage rate in order to compensate the effect of the rising price. We assume that the ratio of wage rate to the planned price w_P / P_{2P} is kept at a constant level for the partial price adjustment.

We will now examine the effects of this kind of policy. If the planned price for consumer goods is raised by ρ percent, the nominal wage rate will also be ρ percent higher. Owing to the fact that the employment can not change in a short period of time in the planned segment, the capital income changes.

For the distribution of the factor income we obtain:

$$(1+\rho)P_{2P}Y_{2P} = (1+\rho)r_{2P}K_{2P} + (1+\rho)w_{2P}L_{2P}$$

Thus the rental rate of capital in the industrial sector will rise at ρ percent, as shown in the equation:

$$r_{2P}^* = (1+\rho)r_{2P}$$

The impact on the market segment is carried out through the deficit of supply of consumer goods. This is expressed as:

$$E = w_P L_P - P_{2P} Y_{2P}$$

As w_P and P_{2P} are increased by ρ percent and the Y_{2P} and L_{2P} are unchanged, shortage of supply will increase by the same percentage. For the wage rate in the market segment, we assume a instantaneous adjustment of w_{2M} to w_P so that $w_{2M} = v_E w_P$ still holds, i.e. w_{2M} increases also by ρ percent. From the equation (10m*) we can easily see that the rising price does not affect the labour intensities in the two sectors of the market segment. The left hand side of the minimum wage condition (10m*) is independent of the decision of the planned segment and the right hand side remains constant if the wage-price-ratio remains unchanged:

$$f_2(l_2) u_2(l_1) \left(\frac{1}{f_{2M}} - \frac{1}{\delta_E} \right) = \frac{Y_{2P}}{K_M} \left(\frac{1}{\delta_E} - \frac{P_{2P}}{v_E w_P} \right) \qquad (10m^*)$$

According to the relationship between the labour intensities and the wage-rental ratio, (1ma) and (2ma), the rental rate in the market segment and the wage rate in agriculture rise by ρ percent. In equations (7ma) and (8ma) the market prices also rise by ρ percent.

All in all, the partial price adjustment causes a rise in all monetary variables by ρ percent, while the real variables remain unchanged so that the allocation of resources and the difference between the growth rate also remain unchanged. In this context, the wage rate can be treated as the Walrasian numéraire in our model[65].

5.6.2 Dual Prices

The "two-tiers system" is another variant of the price reform. According to the „two-tiers system", the state-owned enterprises must fulfil certain plan targets. A certain amount of products have to be produced and sold at the planned price, but the enterprises are free to dispose of the remaining products and their profit, after they have met the planned targets. This policy has brought new light to the management of the state-owned enterprises. The executives become more and more conscious of interests of their enterprises. Of course, it takes time for the executives of the state-owned enterprises to take advantage of this constrained freedom in management and to adjust the production accordingly. We will discuss two cases. In the first case, production is determined independently from the market price, thus somethat exogenous. In the second case, the amount above

---

[65]Brems, Hans. (1968), "Quantitative Economic Theory: A Synthetic Approach",John Wiley & Sons,Inc. New York, London, and Sydney, 1968, p.256

the plan is determined in accordance with the market situation (For simplicity we assume: $s_r = 1$ and $s_w = 0$).

For the first case:

$$Y_{2P} = Y_{2P}^P + Y_{2P}^+ \qquad Y_{2P}^P = I_{2P}^P + C_{2P}^P \qquad Y_{2P}^+ = I_{2P}^+ + C_{2P}^+$$

with $Y_{2P}^P, I_{2P}^P, C_{2P}^P$: the planned target; $Y_{2P}^+, I_{2P}^+, C_{2P}^+$: the amount over the planned target and Y_{2P}: the total amount of production.

$$P_{2P} Y_{2P}^P + P_{2M} Y_{2P}^+ = r_P K_P + w_P L_P$$

The shortage of supply in the planned portion is expressed as:

$$E = w_P L_P - P_{2P} Y_{2P}^P$$

The market balance for consumer goods is:

$$P_{2M}(C_{2M} + C_{2P}^+) = w_{2M} L_{2M} + w_{1M} L_{1M} + E - P_{1M} Y_{1M}.$$

The market balance for investment goods is:

$$P_{2M}(I_{2M} + I_{2P}^+) = r_M K_M + r_P K_P - P_{2P} I_{2P}^P,$$

or

$$P_{2M} I_{2M} = r_M K_M + P_{2M} C_{2M}^+ - E.$$

This equation can be restated in intensive form:

$$P_{2M} \delta_1 u_2 f_2 = r_M - e + P_{2M} c_P^+ \qquad \text{with } c_P^+ = \frac{C_{2P}^+}{K_M}$$

The shares of capital stock in the two sectors η_1 and η_2 can be determined in the following equation:

$$\eta_1 = \frac{r_M - e}{u_2 P_{2M} f_2} + \frac{c_P^+}{u_2 f_2}$$

$$\eta_2 = 1 - \eta_1$$

The minimum wage condition is now given as:

$$w_{2M} = \delta_E \left(\frac{Y_{2P}^P}{Y_{2P}^P + Y_{2P}^+ + Y_{2M}} P_{2P} + \frac{Y_{2P}^+ + Y_{2M}}{Y_{2P}^P + Y_{2P}^+ + Y_{2M}} P_{2M} \right),$$

and the condition for the existence of equilibrium is expressed as:

$$(f_2 u_2 P_{2M} + P_{2M} Y_{2P}^+ / K_M)(1 - \frac{f_2'}{\delta_E}) = \frac{Y_{2P}}{K_M}(\frac{w_M}{\delta_E} - P_{2P}) \tag{10m-c}$$

Because Y_{2P}^+ / K_M is constant, the left hand side of equation (10m-c) monotonously increases in r_M. The conclusion that the equilibrium solution exits uniquely will not change. We denote the left hand side with $D°(r_M)$:

$$D°(r_M) = (f_2 u_2 + Y_{2P}^+ / K_M)(\frac{w_{2M}}{f_2'} - \frac{w_{2M}}{\delta_E}) = D(r_M) + (Y_{2P}^+ / K_M)(\frac{w_{2M}}{f_2'} - \frac{w_{2M}}{\delta_E})$$

Obviously it holds that $D°(r_M) > D(r_M)$ and $D°(r_M)' > D(r_M)'$. This means that the equilibrium rental rate of capital will be smaller, if all other conditions remain unchanged.

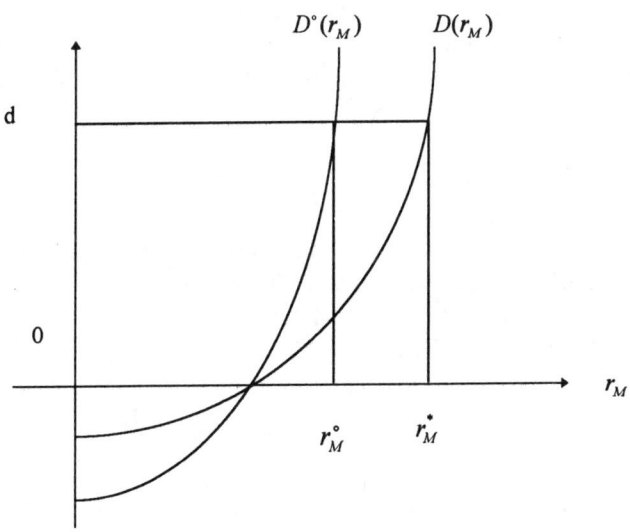

Graph 5.3 Existence of Equilibrium under Two-Tiers-System

Under the dual price system, the state-owned enterprises could also profit from the liberal economic environment through selling part of their products at a higher market price. More production capacity is involved in market-oriented production so that the rental rate in the market segment decreases. (See **Graph 5.3**) Due to the higher price of the product, the rental rate increases in the planned segment. In spite of this, the rental rate in the market segment is still higher than that in the planned segment. Therefore, the growth rate is higher in the market segment.

In the case of endogenous production, where production in the planned segment is determined according to the market prices of the products, the equations for the system remain the same, whereas Y_{2P}^+ / K_M is no longer exogenous. It is determined according to the market situation. Generally, the over-plan-production is determined so that the real wage rate is equal to the marginal labour productivity.

$$F_{2P}'(K_{2P}, L_{2P}) = \frac{w_P}{P_{2M}}$$

or

$$f_{2P}'(l_{2P}) = \frac{w_P}{P_{2M}}$$

Because marginal productivity is a decreasing function, the labour intensity increases along with the market price. The labour intensity in the planned segment can be hence seen as an increasing function of the wage-price ratio:

$$l_{2P} = l_{2P}\left(\frac{w_P}{P_{2M}}\right)$$

The market price increases with the rental rate in the market segment; the labour intensity in the planned segment increases with the rental rate. As the capital stock remains constant, over-plan-production is an increasing function of r_M. We denote the left hand side of equation (10m-c) as $D^{\triangleright}(r_{2M})$. $D^{\triangleright}(r_{2M})$ still monotonously increases in r_M. There exists therefore a unique solution to the equilibrium problem, which is expressed in the equation below (See **Graph 5.3b**):

$$D^{\triangleright}(r_M) = (f_2 u_2 + Y_{2P}^+ (l_{2P}(\frac{w_P}{f_2'}) / K_M)(\frac{w_{2M}}{f_2'} - \frac{w_{2M}}{\delta_E})$$

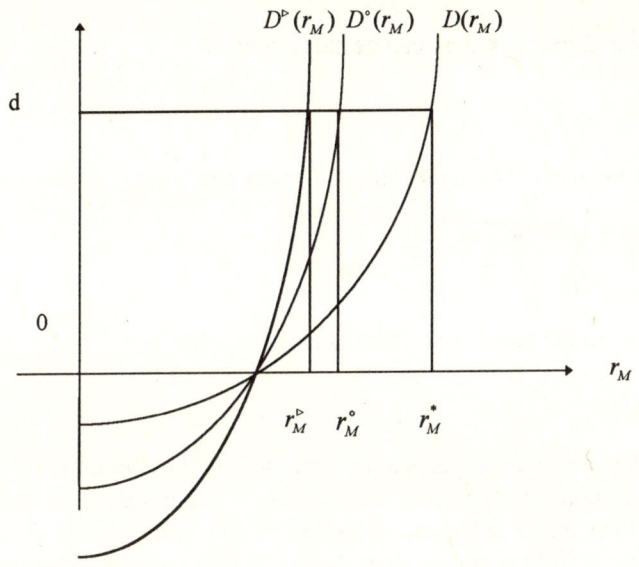

Graph 5.3b Existence of equilibrium under two-tiers-system

5.6.3 Freeing up the Price Control

The last step in the price reform is to give up the planned price and let all prices respond freely to the supply and demand of the market. The practice of this policy may be viewed as continuation of the two-tiers-policy, as the planned portion becomes smaller and smaller. In this case, the minimum wage condition takes a very simple form:

$$w_{2M} = \delta_E P_{2M}$$

This shows that even if all prices are „set free", the wage-price-ratio can not become arbitrarily small. δ_E is the minimum real consumption level, which is determined by the social background.

The equilibrium rental rate in the market segment can be solved in the following equation:

$$f'(l_2) = \delta_E = \frac{w_{2M}}{P_{2M}}.$$

Employment in the market segment can be calculated as:

$$L_{2P} = l_{2P} K_{2P},$$

where the labour intensity should meet the following condition:

$$f_{2P}'(l_{2P}) = \frac{w_{2P}}{P_{2M}} = \frac{w_{2M}/v_E}{P_{2M}} = \delta_E / v_E.$$

The disequilibrium in the planned segment is expressed by:

$$E = w_P L_P - P_{2M} C_{2P}$$

As long as the planned segment plays a dominant role in the economy, we assume that the deficit of supply for consumption is positive. Because the production in the planned segment does not respond to the market situation, it would be a coincidence for the E to be equal to zero. However, the resource allocation in the market segment will react to this disequilibrium and keep the whole economy in equilibrium.

Since planned prices are the foundation of the planning calculation, abolishing the price control is like giving up the entire planned economy. Without the planned price as a basis of evaluation of the target, it is impossible to control or judge, whether the plan is carried out well or not. The practicability of the plan is now very questionable. The planned segment is no longer a subsystem, which could function independently. The dependence of the planned segment on the market changes the role of the planned segment in the economy qualitatively.

The direct effect of abandoning price control is that the difference in the growth rates is reduced as the price advantage of the market segment diminishes. The planned segment obtains more vitality and can grow faster than before. Without price control, the enterprises in the planned segment operate under a more market-like environment and gain more and more market-specific features. The intrinsic transition takes place. The most far-reaching influence of this policy is the dissolution of the planning mechanism. Because a strict control of the execution of the plan strongly depends on information about the prices, this price reform policy made control impossible.

The impact of „freeing up" prices in the whole economy is tremendous. However, this policy may have different results at different times throughout the transition.

At a certain stage in the transition process, this policy could promote the development of the market segment, in another stage of the transition, it could even block the transition process. Correct timing is crucial for this policy (see 5.11).

5.7 Advantages in the Market Segment

In an economy with two subsystems organised by different principles, the vitality of a subsystem could be judged on the rate of growth of that subsystem. Generally, the ratio of the growth rate can be written as:[66]

$$\frac{\rho_P}{\rho_M} = \frac{r_P}{r_M} = \frac{P_P H_P(w_P/P_P)}{P_M H_M(w_M/P_M)}$$

In this formula the advantage in the market segment in regard to the rate of growth of the capital stock can be traced back to three advantages in the market segment. The first is the price advantage. Producers from the market segment can take advantage of the shortage situation and always sell their products at a higher price. It holds that $P_M > P_P$. The second is the wage advantage. Owing to the large labour reserve in agriculture, the industrial enterprises in the market segment face an almost unlimited labour supply, especially at the beginning of the transition when the demand for labour is relatively small. They can therefore hire the labour at lower wage rate $w_M < w_P$. The last advantage is a more efficient production. In the previous discussion, we assumed that production technologies are the same in both segments. There are some good reasons why production in the market segment is more efficient than that in the planned segment. The most important one is the selectivity of investment: The enterprises in the market segment do not need to cover every branch of the economy. They produce only in the most profitable branches through selective investment, while the enterprises in the planned economy have to cover all the branches, where some production is unprofitable. Consequently, with the same amount of resources, more goods and service can be produced in the market segment than in the planned segment. Better management is another important reason for more efficient production in the market segment.

These three aspects can also be stated in another way: the difference in the growth rates between the two segments consists of the difference in prices, the difference in production technologies, which is expressed through the function g_P

---

[66] We neglect the depreciation in the following discussion to simplify the discussion, because its effects on the two segments do not change the relative advantage/disadvantage of any segment.

and g_M, and the difference in labour intensities, which are expressed separately by l_P and l_M:

$$\frac{\rho_P}{\rho_M} = \frac{r_P}{r_M} = \frac{P_P(f_P(l_P) - f_P'(l_P)l_P)}{P_M(f_M(l_M) - f_M'(l_M)l_M)} = \frac{P_P g_P(l_P)}{P_M g_M(l_M)} \qquad (D)$$

with: $g(l) := f(l) - f'(l)l$

If the production technology is the same in both segments, the difference resulting from labour intensity can be illustrated in the following graph:

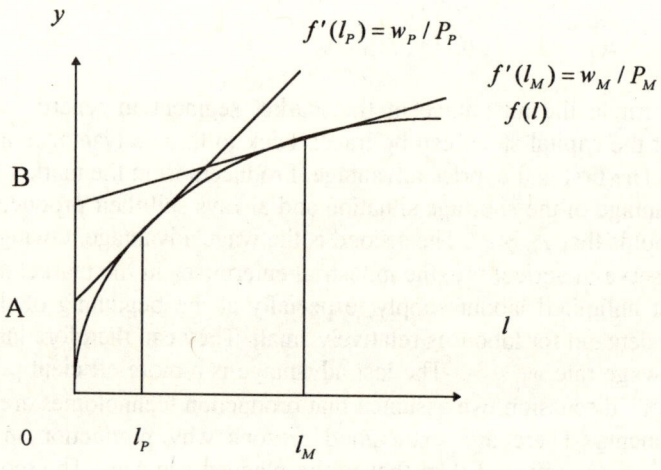

Graph 5.4 Production and labour intensity with same technology

The curve is the production function $f(l)$. From the cost minimising behaviour of the producers we have: $f'(l) = w/P$. Owing to the fact that the wage rate in the market segment is lower than that in the planned segment, the labour intensity in the market segment must be higher than that in the planned segment. Graphically, the slope at l_P must be steeper than that at l_M. l_P is smaller than l_M, because this slope decreases. The intercept can be expressed as: $f - f'l$, which is equal to $g(l)$ by definition. The difference between the intercepts A-B expresses the difference in growth of the capital stock due to the difference in labour intensity (see **Graph 5.4**).

If production in the market segment is more efficient, the difference will be even larger. It is expressed by A-C, which is the sum of the difference due to the labour intensity A-B and the difference due to the production function itself, B-C.

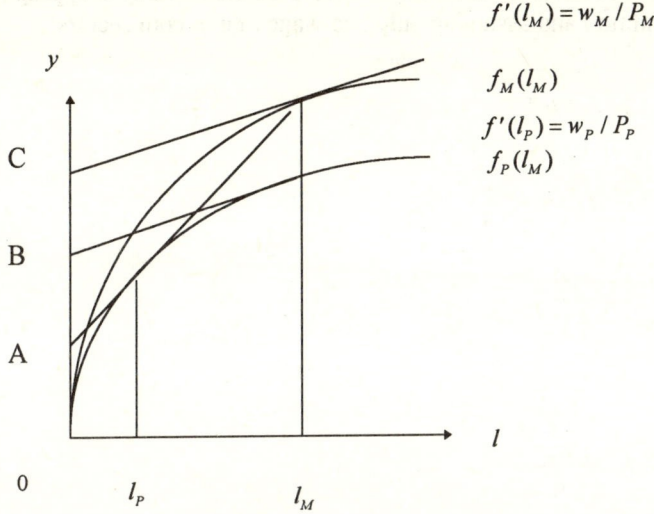

Graph 5.5 Production and labour Intensity with different technologies

During the transition process, the productive capacity of the market segment grows and the behaviour in the planned segment changes. Thus, the relative advantages of the market segment become increasingly weaker with time. Whether the advantage will disappear depends on whether the planned segment will have the same performance as the market segment.

5.8 Industrialisation and Labour Distribution

The previous discussions were conducted under the assumption of labour surplus. The urban minimum wage exceeds the competitive level and draws rural labour into the industrial sector. The industrial sector faces an „unlimited supply of labour", and the minimum wage can prevail. Labourers are engaged in three groups of employment: industrial production in the planned segment, industrial production in the market segment, and agricultural production. During the transition from plan to market, the industrialisation process continues. The labour movement from the agricultural sector into the industrial sector proceeds continuously. Consequently, the agricultural wage rate rises and approaches the industrial wage rate. The living standard in the rural areas improves with the rising labour income in agriculture. When the wage rate in the agricultural sector reaches the level in the industrial sector, a qualitative change in the labour market takes place. There is no longer a labour surplus. The unified real wage rate is no longer fixed on the minimum level but is determined endogenously on the competitive level. The basic model should be modified by dropping the minimum wage condition and assuming only one wage rate in both sectors:

$$f_1/f_1' - l_1 = \frac{r_M}{w_M} \tag{1me}$$

$$f_2/f_2' - l_2 = \frac{r_M}{w_M} \tag{2me}$$

$$u_1 = \frac{e l^*}{f_1(l_1)} \tag{3me}$$

$$\eta_1 u_1 f_2 = r_M - e \tag{4me}$$

$$P_{2M} = \frac{w_M}{f_2'} \tag{5me}$$

$$P_{1M} = \frac{w_M}{f_1'} \tag{6me}$$

$$l_{1M} u_1 + l_{2M} u_2 = l_M = \frac{L_M}{K_M} \tag{7me}$$

As we have previously discussed, all endogenous variables can be viewed as a function of the rent-wage ratio. In the equation (7me) this ratio can be determined. The question of the existence of the solution is whether or not a positive r_M exits, which can meet the equation (7me). To answer this question, we will first show that the left hand side of (7me) is an increasing function of the rental wage ratio r_M/w_M. We denote the left side of (7me) by $G(r_M/w_M)$.

$$dG(\frac{r_M}{w_M}) = d(u_1 l_1 + u_2 l_2) = ((1-u_1)l_2' + u_1(1-f_1'(l_1-l_2)/f_1)l_1')d(\frac{r_M}{w_M}) > 0$$

Hence, $G(r_M/w_M)$ is a rising function of $r_M/w_M r$. Because $\lim_{r_M \to \infty} G(r_M/w_M) = \infty$ and $\lim_{r_M \to 0} G(r_M/w_M) = 0$, a positive $(r_M/w_M)^*$ exists for which $G(r_M/w_M)^* = l_M$.

As the growth of capital stock is much faster than the growth of labour (we have assumed a constant labour supply), the overall labour intensity decreases with time and so does the rental-wage ratio. From the equation (5me) we know that the price of industrial products also decreases. This process goes on until the market price falls below the planned price. From this point on, the planned segment is forced to follow the market price, otherwise no one would buy the products at the planned price. In this case, the planned segment obviously could not survive within the system if it does not adjust itself to the market situation.

The consideration above suggests the conclusion, that industrialisation might be crucial to the transition from plan to market. As soon as the industrialisation process is complete, the thorough removal of the planned segment is inevitable, with the single exception that the planned segment behaves just like the market segment.

The degree of industrialisation can be expressed through the share of industrial products in the whole economy. We have constructed the growth process in our model through the accumulation of capital stock. The entire production grows with time. The industrialisation becomes a direct result of the assumption concerning the dualistic structure of the economy.

5.9 Reform of the Labour Market

Reform of the labour market was, beside the price reform, another important field of the urban reform. Before the economic reform, Chinese were strictly divided into urban residents and rural residents through a bureaucratic command system[67]. „In this kind of command system, labour is just one of the several inputs into production and is handled in many respects like the other inputs."[68] Only the urban residents were provided with employment in the industrial sector. The wage rate in the industrial enterprises was strictly controlled by the planning authority, in order to maintain a high accumulation rate. Those employed in the industrial enterprises, especially in the state-owned enterprises, enjoyed a highly subsided social welfare benefit[69]. The living standard in the urban area was hence higher than in the rural area.

During the reform there is evidence that the market force played an increasingly important role in the wage determination, especially in the market segment[70]. In this section, we are going to incorporate the reform of the labour market into the model and discuss its impact on the transition from plan to market. If the labour market is „set free", both employment and the wage rate are determined by the market mechanism. We have to abandon the equation (11ma) in the basic model. Now that there is no institutional constraint with respect to the nominal wage rate, the wage rate must be equal in the industrial and agricultural sector. However,

---

[67]Compare Willianm L. Parish(1991),P.3-16
[68]Perkins, Dwight H. (1991) p.79 ff.
[69]For details see Cheng, Xuan(1991) p.70 ff.
[70]For detail discussion in this field see Grant Blank, William Parish, Sen-Dou Chang, R Yin-Wang Kwok, and Shen Guanbao (1991)'What Model Now: China Urban Reform'

considering the difference in living cost between the urban and the rural areas, we assume that:

$$w_{1M} = w_{2M} - c(\overline{P}_2).$$

$c(\overline{P}_2)$ stands for the extra living costs in the urban area. $c(\overline{P}_2)$ is a linear homogenous function of the average industrial price. $c(\overline{P}_2)$ would vanish if the industrialisation process would develop so far, that the difference in the social infrastructure between urban and rural area would become negligible. Now we can construct the submodel of the market segment by replacing the equation (11ma) in the basic model with the above equation.

$$f_1 / f_1' - l_1 = \frac{r_M}{w_{1M}} = \omega_1 \tag{1mf}$$

$$f_2 / f_2' - l_2 = \frac{r_M}{w_{2M}} = \omega_2 \tag{2mf}$$

$$u_1 = \frac{el^*}{f_1(l_1)} \tag{3mf}$$

$$u_1 + u_2 = 1 \tag{4mf}$$

$$\eta_1 u_1 f_2 = r_M - e \tag{5mf}$$

$$\eta_1 + \eta_2 = 1 \tag{6mf}$$

$$P_{2M} = \frac{w_{2M}}{f_2'} \tag{7mf}$$

$$P_{1M} = \frac{w_{1M}}{f_1'} \tag{8mf}$$

$$l_1 u_1 + l_2 u_2 = l_M = \frac{L_M}{K_M} \tag{9mf}$$

$$w_{2M} = \delta_E \overline{P}_2 = \delta_E(\lambda P_{2P} + (1-\lambda)P_{2M}) \tag{10mf}$$

$$w_{1M} = w_{2M} - c(\overline{P}_2) \tag{11mf}$$

This submodel consists of 11 independent equations, with which we can solve for the 11 variables of the market segment: $l_1, l_2, P_{1M}, P_{2M}, u_1, u_2, \eta_1, \eta_2, r_M, w_{1M}, w_{2M}$.

The existence and uniqueness of the equilibrium solution can be argued in a similar way as in section 5.8. In equations (10mf) and (11mf) we find a relation between the wage rates in the market segment.

$$w_{1M} = w_{2M} - c(\bar{P}_2) = \delta_E \bar{P}_2 - c(\bar{P}_2) = (\delta_E - c(\bar{P}_2)/\bar{P}_2)\bar{P}_2 = \delta_{AE} \bar{P}_2$$

Because $c(\bar{P}_2)$ is a linear homogenous function of $\bar{P}_2$, $c(\bar{P}_2)/\bar{P}_2$ is independent from $\bar{P}_2$. Therefore, we have:

$$w_{1M} = \frac{\delta_{AE}}{\delta_E} w_{2M} = \lambda_w w_{2M}$$

Using the above relation, we obtain:

$$\omega_1 = \frac{r_M}{w_{1M}} = \frac{r_M}{\lambda_w w_{2M}} = \frac{1}{\lambda_w} \omega_2.$$

As argued in section 5.8, l_1, u_1, u_2 and l_2 can be treated as functions of ω_1. The right hand side of (9mf) is thus a monotone increasing function of ω_1. Hence, a positive ω_1^* can be uniquely determined in the equation (9mf)[71]. Thus all the real variables and the relative prices in the market segment can be determined according to ω_1^*. Owing to the endogenous determination of the wage rate in the market segment, the relative independence of the market segment becomes even stronger. The nominal level of the prices can be determined through equation (10mf). Inserting equation (7mf) in equation (10mf), we obtain:

$$\frac{P_{2P}}{P_{2M}} = \left(\frac{f_2'(\omega_1^*)}{\delta_E} - (1-\lambda) \right) \frac{1}{\lambda}. \qquad (10\text{mf-b})$$

Whether a positive P_{2M} exits, depends on whether the following condition is fulfilled.

$$\frac{f_2'(\omega_1^*)}{\delta_E} > 1 - \lambda \qquad (11\text{mf})$$

---

[71] The sufficient condition for the existence of a positive solution is $f_1'(l_M) > \varepsilon l_G$, which means simply that if all labour and all capital were invested in agriculture, the food production would be enough for the entire population.

If it is fulfilled, there then exists a positive price P_{2M}. If not, there is no positive solution for equation (11mf-b). According to the value of $\frac{f_2'(\omega_1^*)}{\delta_E}$, we can differ among 3 cases in which the property of the model changes qualitatively. Case 1: $\frac{f_2'(\omega_1^*)}{\delta_E} < 1 - \lambda$. δ_E is the minimum consumption level. This inequity implies that the marginal productivity of labour would be far below the minimum consumption level, such that no equilibrium solution for the system under full employment exists. The implication of this solution is that the wage rate in the industrial sector must be fixed on the level of minimum consumption, which is above the competitive level. Therefore, equation (11mf) does not hold in this situation. The wage rate in the agricultural sector must decrease so greatly that the surplus labour force are absorbed by agriculture. This is comparable to the case discussed in chapter 4. Case 2: $1 > \frac{f_2'(\omega_1^*)}{\delta_E} > 1 - \lambda$: We know from the above discussion that the second inequity implies a positive solution for P_{2M} exists. The first inequity implies that the production in the market segment can run with the marginal productivity under the minimum real consumption level of the worker, which would be impossible in any pure market economy. The very reason here is that although labour in the market is priced at a level below the minimum real consumption with respect to the market price, the minimum consumption level can still be reached, evaluated at the average price. In other words, the market segment can take advantage of the lower price in the planned segment and allow itself to pay its employees at a real wage rate under existence minimum with respect to the market price. This case is comparable to the case discussed in section 5.8, with the slight difference that we have taken into consideration the extra living expenses in the urban area, while in section 5.8 the extra living expenses are neglected. Case 3 $\frac{f_2'(\omega_1^*)}{\delta_E} \geq 1$: This inequity implies that $P_{2P} \geq P_{2M}$. In this case the market price is lower that the planned price. The existence of the planned segment would be threatened by the competition from the market segment. The planned segment would be forced to adjust itself to the market situation and to follow the market price. If we take the dynamic aspect into account, the evolution from case 1 to case 3 would follow the growth process in the market segment. We know that at the beginning the capital stock in the market segment is very small and the equilibrium ω_1^* must be at a level with a very large labour intensity. The marginal productivity is therefore also very small at the beginning. Because the capital stock grows faster than the labour force, the equilibrium ω_1^* would decrease with time and the labour intensity would become smaller. Therefore, the marginal productivity rises with the growth process. Along the growth path of the system, it goes from case 1 to case 3.

The function of the model can be stated as follows:
The market segment functions just as a market economy does in a neo-classical equilibrium model (in this case with a dualistic character). The allocation of production factors and relative prices are results of the equilibrium, which is independent from decisions in the planned segment. But the nominal level of the variable is closely connected with the planned price. The planned segment serves here as a supplier with a rigidly lower price. Through the transaction with the planned segment, the market segment can take advantage of this lower price: production can run even under a very low labour productivity. The real wage valued at the market price can even be lower than the existence minimum of the labourer. Therefore, the existence of the planned segment helps the market segment to grow fast at the beginning. It is reasonable to assume that at the beginning the capital stock in the market segment is very small. Hence, the labour productivity, thus the wage rate, is very low in the market segment. A lower wage and a higher price lead to a faster growth of the market segment. Consequently, the wage rate in the market segment rises. As long as the wage rate in the market segment is lower than that in the planned segment and the market price is higher than planned price, the market segment grows faster; the planned segment can still function in its old fashion. The existence of the planned segment is threatened if the market wage rate approaches the planned one and/or the market price becomes close to the planned price. From then on, the planned segment is forced to adjust to the market situation. The transition from plan to market is then inevitable.

If the price is „set free" during the reform of the labour market, the planned price and the market price will then be unified at the level of the market price. $P_{2M} = P_{2P} = \overline{P}_2$. Equation (10mf) should be dropped out of the system. The existence of an equilibrium solution depends on whether or not the marginal productivity in the market segment is above the minimum consumption level. If the marginal productivity of the market segment lies below the minimum consumption level, there is no equilibrium solution for the system. This is typically the case in developing countries, in which a wage level over the competitive level prevails in the industrial sector. Not all labour resource can be utilised in industrial production. The surplus labour has to be absorbed in the agricultural (or traditional) sector. It is then necessary to modify the model. Equation (11mf) should be dropped out of the system and equation (10mf) should be modified as following:

$$w_{2M} = \delta_E \overline{P}_2$$

This is exactly the case as discussed in section 5.6.3.

If the marginal productivity of the market segment lies above the minimum consumption level, i.e. $f(\omega_1^*) > \delta_E$, the equilibrium solution exists uniquely. This is the case similar to that discussed in section 5.8. The wage rate raises during the evolution path. The market segment grows faster until the wage rate reaches the level of the planned wage rate. The wage rate in the planned segment is then forced to adjust to the market situation. The forced adjustment takes place.

5.10 Welfare Effect of Transition

The consumption possibility expressed through real income is taken here as the indicator of welfare. It is well known that the welfare concept is much more comprehensive than just a single object of real income[72]. Constrained by the model structure, the welfare effect will only be examined in this partial aspect. The participants of the economy during the transition process can be roughly divided into 4 groups: farmers, who are engaged in agricultural production, farmer-workers, who were farmers and became industrial workers during the industrialisation process, workers of the state-owned enterprises, and capitalists, who own the capital stocks. The impact of the transition from plan to market on the welfare is different among the four groups because they are engaged differently in the economy.

At the early stage of the economic reform, farmers benefited from the rural reform through the rising price of agricultural products and the „freeing up" of the market for agricultural products and side line products. During the transition process accompanied by the industrialisation process, labourers moved continuously from the agricultural sector to the industrial sector. The marginal productivity increased in agriculture, thus farmers' income rose continuously. Although farmers' income was the lowest among the four groups, farmers were facing improving living standards. Hence, they are happy with the reform policies, as long as the improvement continues.

Farmer-workers improved their living standard by moving to the industrial employment. They earned more than their former colleagues, who remained in the countryside. In this sense, they are grateful to the reform policy. However, they have to lead a rather hard live in the urban area. Owing to the excess supply of labour, their real income is fixed on the minimum level. They faced the fact that although they earned more and they had to spend more for living. Hence, their opinion on the reform is two-fold. On the one hand, they are grateful to the reform policy that they got the chance to work in industry and could thus improve their living standards in comparison to the situation before the reform. On the

---

[72] Sen, Amartya (1988): in Hand Book of Development Economics Vol. 1, P.12 ff.

other hand, they always complain that the reform can not give them further improvements in living standards.

Workers of the state-owned enterprises can not profit directly from the transition process because their wage rate was determined through the central planning. They might suffer from a loss of welfare due to the rising prices, which is caused by the higher prices in the market segment. However, with the progress of reform in the state-owned enterprises, the enterprises have gained comprehensive autonomy. The managers of the enterprises raised the income of the workers through raising the share of premium in the total wage. From 1978 to 1993 the share of the regular wage in the total wage fell from 85.8% to 50%. According to this fact, the central planning did not play the decisive role any longer in wage determination. This naturally raises the question: How is the wage rate determined in the state-owned enterprises during the economic reform? Neither the theory of marginal productivity nor the efficiency wage model can provide a sufficient explanation to this phenomenon, because statistics show that the increase of the wage rate in the state-owned enterprises is larger than the increase of productivity. Obviously, the managers of the state-owned enterprises have taken the growth of the real income of their workers into their object function[73]. These wage increases are partly responsible for the fall of the profit rate in the state-owned enterprises during the transition process. Due to the increased real wage, workers in the state-owned enterprises experienced a welfare gain during the transition. However, it is questionable whether this improvement can last throughout the transition process. The profit fall will threaten the existence of the state-owned enterprises and thus the existence of the workers. Without significant technical progress, the improvement of the living standards of the workers in the state-owned enterprises can not continue during the transition process.

The capitalists have profited the most through the transition process. In the early stages of reform, the capital rental rate was very high. A remarkable process of capital accumulation took place in the market segment during the reform. Along with the capital accumulation a new entrepreneur class slowly forms during the transition process. This class naturally supports the reform policy. The role of small savers, who only deposit their money in the bank, is totally different from the capitalists, who invest money directly in the production process. Due to the monopoly position of the bank, the interest rate is always set at a level not higher than the inflation rate, such that small savers can not profit from their capital - savings.

To sum up, the 4 groups can all profit from the economic reform. Farmers, who earn the least among the four groups, can improve their living standards as long

---

[73] Wing Thye Woo has argued for this behaviour in Wing Thye Woo (1994), P. 286.

as the industrialisation process continues. Farmer-workers, whose income is between farmers and the other group, improve their living standards by moving from the agricultural to the industrial sector. A further improvement is not possible before farmers' income reaches the level of the farmer-workers. From then on their real wage rises continuously. Workers of the state-owned enterprises, who earn the most among the working class, obtain real wage increases because the managers of the state-owned enterprises act partly as an agency of the workers. However, these increases of the real wage are not economically founded. They can only last in the long run if the technical progress in the state-owned enterprises can guarantee enough growth in productivity. The newly-emerged capitalists profit the most during the transition process.

5.11 Timing of the Reform

The evolution path of the model as a series of the temporal equilibrium in the system depends on the initial condition and the functioning mechanism in each period respectively. Any reform policy that is designed to change the function of the planned segment can affect the state of the temporal equilibrium in each period, and thus the process of the transition from plan to market. It is worthy to discuss, whether a certain policy aimed at accelerating the transition from plan to market can really have this expected effect. It turns out that it is crucial whether the ratio of the production capacity of the market segment to that of the planned segment has reached a certain level at the time in which the policy is carried out. Because the ratio of production capacity between the two segments alters with time, the timing of a reform policy may be crucial as to whether or not the policy can have its intended effect.

We know from the discussion in chapter 4, that if the overall economic situation in the system still has CPE-specific features depends on whether or not the market segment can correct the disequilibrium situation produced by the planned segment. The critical point is whether or not the equilibrium rental rate in the market segment is larger than the rate of disequilibrium expressed by E/K_M. If $r_M^* > \frac{E}{K_M}$, the market segment can absorb the disequilibrium. If $r_M^* < \frac{E}{K_M}$, the disequilibrium situation persists and forced savings exist. If forced savings are used for investment in the planned segment, the transition may be stopped. Recalling the conclusion of the discussion about the dual price in the state-owned enterprises (see section 5.6.2), we know that the equilibrium rental rate becomes smaller with the dual price policy. If this policy was introduced at an early stage of the reform when the market production capacity was still very small, the market rental rate might have possibly become smaller than the disequilibrium rate. This might have led to disequilibrium in the whole economy. Even worse, it might have ceased the transition process if the growth of the planned segment supported by forced savings had been faster than that in the market segment. Thus, a policy which is designed to accelerate the transition process may result in the opposite effect. A Similar conclusion holds also for the policy of „freeing up" of price control. However, when the production capacity in the market segment is expanded so far that the disequilibrium rate is far smaller than the market rental rate, the price reform can have its intended effect - enforcing the transition process.

From the above example, we may conclude that in the evaluation of a reform policy we must always consider the interaction between the planned segment and the market segment, even if the policy may only be designed for the planned segment. Correct timing plays an important role in achieving the expected effect.

5.12 Feasible Transition Path

From the previous discussion we have seen that whether or not the transition from plan to market can proceed successfully depends on the constellation of the planned segment and the market segment on the one hand, and policy intervention on the other. The evolution process, driven by the laisser-faire market force, may not always lead to a successful transition from plan to market (section 4.4). Besides production technology and the practice in the planned segment, the ratio of the production capacity in the market segment to that in the planned segment is crucial for the transition process. To promote the transition, the policy-makers are asked to create a sound initial condition for the transition through political measures. The reform policy, aimed at transforming the planned segment into the market segment, such as price reform and wage reform and labour market reform, does not always lead to acceleration of the transition process. Under certain circumstances, it could be an obstacle to the transition process, if these policies were not carried out with appropriate timing. However, numerous political options exist which could lead to a successful end of the transition.

Although the evolution path depends on the initial condition and the political intervention and is hence not unique, the development of the economic system goes through several similar stages along each feasible successful transition path.

At the early stage, when the market segment comes into existence, the capital stock of the market segment is rather small. Its production is restricted at first to the consumption sector. The unsatisfied demand for consumer goods provides a ready market for the products. The production of consumer goods is technically less complicated than the production of investment goods so that the new producers may have an easy start in the consumer sector. Moreover, the production of consumer products is desired by the reform policy-makers, who are anxious to improve the supply situation in the consumption market.

Through the appearance of the market segment in the economy, the supply situation is improved. The labour force moved to the industrial production. The whole economy grows faster and becomes more flexible in production and resource allocation. Owing to the insufficient production capacity in the market segment, not all the deficit in the supply of consumer goods can be covered. The unsatisfied consumer demand becomes forced saving. The planned segment is still dominant in the economy. The main features of the CPE in the economy, such as shortage of supply, fixed prices and rigid factor allocation, are only quantitatively reduced. However, the big difference between the demand and the supply due to the insufficient production capacity drives the market price to its highest level. The price advantage of the market segment is at its greatest. Hence, the market segment grows faster at this stage. In general, the market segment plays a complimentary role in the economy. We call this stage the complimentary stage.

The second stage begins when production in the market segment expands into the investment sector. During the first stage, a certain production capacity was established in the market segment. It can cover the whole supply deficit of the planned segment. Moreover, the enterprises in the market segment are also involved in the production of investment goods. The market segment becomes more and more an independent economic sub-system. While during the first stage the market segment has to rely on the investment products from the planned segment, it can now, at least in part, cover the demand for investment production through its own production.

During this stage, the growth rate in the market segment is larger than that in the planned segment. The price advantage, the wage advantage, and the production advantage support faster growth in the market segment. Of course, with the expansion of the market segment the price advantage is reduced step by step. But, the price advantage continues to be significant throughout this stage. The overall economic situation is much more market-like. The features of the CPE exist only within the planned segment and are not significant for the whole economy any longer. In this stage, both the planned segment and the market segment show development. The transition is taking place. We call this stage the development stage.

Facing faster growth in the market segment and shrinking share of the planned segment in the economy, the policy makers are motivated to carry out reform to adjust the planned segment to the new economic situation. We have discussed various reform policies in the previous sections. All the policies are aimed at accelerating growth in the planned segment by making it more market-like. These adjustments imply the reduction of the central plan step by step and even abandoning the central planning completely. These adjustments can lower the price advantage, the production advantage and the wage advantage of the market segment. However, these advantages can only be completely neutralised if all the planning decisions in the planned segment coincide with those in the market segment. This implies, however, that the planned segment would itself become a market segment. The policy-making in this stage of the transition concentrates on the adjustment of the planned segment to catch up to the advantages of the market segment. We call this stage the voluntary adjustment stage.

Parallel to the transition process, the industrialisation process continues. The labour movement takes place continuously. With the increasing productivity in agriculture, the wage difference between industry and agriculture becomes smaller. The labour surplus reduces with time. The fourth stage begins when the labour surplus disappears. In further development, the real wage in the market segment rises. As soon as the real wage in the market segment reaches that in the planned segment, the competition from the market segment threatens the existence of the planned segment. The planned segment can only survive in the system if it performs just the same as the market segment. This implies that the planned segment itself has to become a market segment. Hence, we call this stage the forced adjustment stage.

Chapter 6

Numerical Studies and Empirical Relevance

In Chapter 5, we discussed that the transition is driven by the built-in market mechanism of the economy with interaction between the planned and the market segment. Since economic policies can influence decisions in the planned segment and the initial market conditions can affect the equilibrium state, it is of interest to analyse changes in the transitional path in dependence on the alternative reform policies and different market conditions such as production technology, population growth, saving behaviour, and so on. Numerical simulation provides a suitable instrument for this kind of analysis. Because there are so many factors that can influence the evolution path of the system, it is impossible to study a complete set of alternative policies and different market constellations. Therefore, we will choose a basic evolution path of the system and the analysis of alternative paths will be carried out in comparison to this basic path. The focus here concentrates on only a few interesting policies that might be relevant to the practice. Beyond that, we will simulate the realised path in light of the theoretical model. To be verified is whether or not the model can give a proper description of the reality with initial values and parameters chosen somewhat „correctly". A more sound way for such studies would be to impose some sophisticated econometric methods on the model and to estimate the parameters. Unfortunately, not all the needed statistical materials are available. Moreover, observations of some important variables do not even exist. We have to rely on the theoretical arguments and some conclusions in related literature in choosing of parameters.

6.1. Choice of Parameters and Initial Values

In numerical studies, the evolution of the system is calculated iteratively. At first, we choose initial values (such as the capital stock and the population) to begin an iteration. According to these initial values, the decisions of the planned segment and the equilibrium solution of the system will be computed from the static equations of the model. With the result of the equilibrium solution, we can update the starting values for the next period using the dynamic equations of the model. This computational process then goes on iterativly. The equilibrium solution in each period constitutes the evolutionary path of the system. The following graph shows this computational process.

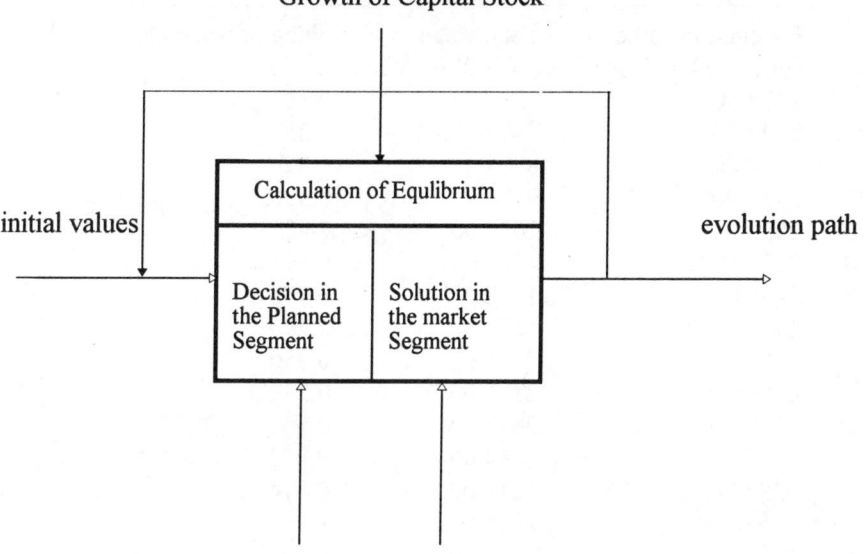

6.1.1 Determination of the Parameters:

1) Parameters for production functions:

For simplicity, we will use Cobb-Douglas-production[76] functions for both industrial and agricultural productions.

$$Y_{1M} = \gamma_1 K_{1M}^{\alpha_1} L_{1M}^{\beta_1} \qquad Y_{2M} = \gamma_2 K_{2M}^{\alpha_2} L_{2M}^{\beta_2} \qquad Y_{2P} = \gamma_2 K_{2P}^{\alpha_2} L_{2P}^{\beta_2}$$

Under the assumption of the cost minimising behaviour of producers, β_2 would be roughly estimated according to the share of the labour income in the total production value.

---

[76]The same studies have also been carried out with a CES-production function. The result does not alter essentially.

Table 6.1 Share of labour income[77]

Year	Production value (in 100 Min. Yuan)	Total wage (in 100Min. Yuan)	Share of wage income
1978	2024.00	654.00	0.323
1979	2124.00	749.00	0.352
1980	2362.00	890.00	0.376
1981	2432.00	949.00	0.390
1982	2535.00	1034.00	0.407
1983	2815.00	1109.00	0.393
1984	3401.00	1368.00	0.402
1985	4528.00	1677.00	0.370
1986	5139.00	1985.00	0.386
1987	6159.00	2295.00	0.372
1988	7920.00	2835.00	0.357
1989	8967.00	3164.00	0.352
1990	9384.00	3511.00	0.374
1991	11288.00	3959.00	0.350
1992	14050.00	4783.00	0.340

Source : Chinese Statistic Year Book 1993 p.33, p.128, p.121 and p.397.

The empirical data in Table 6.1 show, that this share is rather constant over time between 1978 and 1992. Hence, we choose $\beta_2=0.4$ and $\alpha_2=0.6$. Unfortunately, we do not have any reliable statistics for the share of labour income in agricultural production. It is practically impossible to split the production income of the family-based agricultural production into capital income and labour income. We have to rely on theoretical arguments[78] and other comparable statistics. Because the value of materials used in agricultural production is between 20% and 30% of the total production value[79], we assume that $\alpha_1=0.25$ and $\beta_1=0.75$. In the numerical study we will alter these coefficients to account for other possible parameters. The values of γ_1 and γ_2 depend on the chosen units, in which the products and the production factors are measured. They can be determined as follows:

$$\gamma_i = \frac{Y_i}{K_i^{\alpha_i} L_i^{\beta_i}}.$$

---

[77]The Production value is the total national income minus the income from agriculture. The total wage is the sum of wage income in the state-owned enterprises, in the collective enterprises, and in the village-township enterprises.
[78]The agriculture production is much more labour intensive than the industrial production and in our model the income in the agricultural in lower than in the industry. This implies that the relation $\beta_2/\alpha_2 < \beta_2/\alpha_2$ must be hold.
[79]See Statistic Year Book 1988 p.58.

According to statistics, the net value of industrial production in 1978 was 148.7 (billion yuan). About ¾ was produced in state-owned enterprises. Total employment in state-owned enterprises was 74 million. Hence we may obtain[80]:

$\gamma_2 = \dfrac{0.75 \cdot 148.7}{600^{0.6} \cdot 0.074^{0.4}} \approx 7$. For agricultural production we may obtain[81]:

$\gamma_1 = \dfrac{0.3}{30^{0.25} \cdot 0.306^{0.75}} = 0.75$. The coefficient of depreciation is chosen to be 0.05.

2) Parameters for saving and consumption:

The per capita demand for agricultural products can be calculated from the ratio of the agricultural production to the total labour force.

Table 6.2 Average consumption of grain[82]

Year	Grain (in 10000. T.) (1)	Total labourers (in 10000) (2)	Average consumption of grain (2)/(3)
1978	30477	40152	0,75
1979	33212	41024	0,80
1980	32056	42361	0,75
1981	32502	43725	0,74
1982	35450	45295	0,78
1983	38728	46436	0,83
1984	40731	48197	0,84
1985	37911	49873	0,76
1986	39151	51282	0,76
1987	40298	52783	0,76
1988	39408	54334	0,72
1989	40755	55329	0,73
1990	44624	56740	0,78
1991	43529	58360	0,74
1992	44266	59432	0,74
1993	45648	60220	0,75
1994	44510	61470	0,72

Source: Chinese Statistic Year Book 1995 p.85 and p.347

---

[80] For the production value See Statistic Year Book 1988 p.51 for the ratio of state owned enterprises see Statistic Year Book 1993 p.412.
[81] For the amount of agriculture production see statistic year book 1988 pp 248; for the labour force employed in the agriculture see p.153. The capital assets are estimated.
[82] Grain is measured in 10 thousand tons and labour in 10 thousand.

From **Table 6.2** we can see that this ratio is almost constant over a period from 1978 to 1994. We choose: $\varepsilon = \frac{Y_1}{L_G} = 0.75$.

If we take the average wage of state-owned enterprises in 1978 as the planned wage rate, then $w_P=630$ (see **Table 6.9**). The difference between the wage rates in state-owned enterprises and non-state-owned enterprises is shown in Table 6.9. Hence, we assume that the ratio between the wage rates is $v_E=0.7$, thus $w_M = 440$[83]. For the saving fraction we assume S_r lies between 0.7 and 0.9 and S_w between 0.05 and 0.15[84]. In numerical studies, we will change the fraction to take various saving fractions into account.

3) The initial values:

Initial values include the amount of capital stocks in both segments and the total labour force at the beginning of the transition process. We will choose the capital stock from the existing statistics Kp=6000[85](in 100 million Yuan). There is, however, not any information about the capital stocks in non-state owned enterprises. We assume, that the capital stock in the market segment is at the beginning much smaller than that in the planned segment. The impact of different starting capital stocks on the whole transition process can be examined through alternative values for the starting capital stocks. In the basic path we assume Km=1000. For the total labour force at the beginning we use the data from the statistics: Lg=4 (in hundred million)[86].

4) External dynamics

The dynamic property of the model is determined through capital accumulation, technological progress, and growth of population. While the capital accumulation is endogenously determined in the equilibrium, the technical process and the growth in population are treated in the model as exogenous variables. In order to take the growth of population and technological progress into account, we have to

---

[83]Because the minimum consumption level can expressed as the ratio of wage to average price, it can be calculated by choosing average price. We assume in the model that the average price is 10% higher than the planned price.

[84]The saving fraction of the labour income can be roughly calculated as the ratio of the increment of saving in the cities to the total wage income. (See Statistic Year Book 1987 pp. 805 p.177. This ratio is an over estimation in the later period of the economic reform, because then the saving of capital income may also partially be included in this statistic.

[85]Here Kp is the sum of fixed capital assets and flowing capital assets of the state-owned enterprises. See Statistic Yea Book p.33 and 34.

[86]See Statistic Year Book 1988 p.153.

formulate two exogenous dynamic processes to model the growth in population and the change of production technology.
For simplicity we assume, that the population is growing at a constant rate:

$$Lg(t+1)=(1+\rho_L)Lg(t).$$

and technological progress can be modeled as:

$$\gamma_i = \gamma_0 e^{\lambda_i t}.$$

6.1.2 The Simulation model

Production in the planned segment:

$$Y_{2P} = \gamma_2 K_{2P}^{\alpha_2} L_{2P}^{\beta_2} \qquad (1p)$$
$$Y_{1M} = \gamma_1 K_{1M}^{\alpha_1} L_{1M}^{\beta_1} \qquad (1m)$$
$$Y_{2M} = \gamma_2 K_{2M}^{\alpha_2} L_{2M}^{\beta_2} \qquad (2m)$$

Composition of industrial production:

$$Y_{2P} = I_{2P} + C_{2P} \qquad (2p)$$
$$Y_{2M} = I_{2M} + C_{2M} \qquad (3m)$$

Inflexibility of the composition in the planned segment:

$$\frac{I_{2P}}{C_{2P}} = \mu \qquad (2p)$$

Factor demand:

a) Before the price reform:
$$\frac{\partial F_{2P}}{\partial L_{2P}} = \frac{w_P}{P_{2P}} \qquad (3p)$$

b) After the price reform:
$$\frac{\partial F_{2P}}{\partial L_{2P}} = \frac{w_P}{P_{2M}}. \qquad (3p\text{-}b)$$
$$\frac{\partial F_{2P}}{\partial K_{2P}} = \frac{r_P}{P_{2M}} \qquad (4p)$$
$$\frac{\partial F_{iM}}{\partial K_{iM}} = \frac{r_M}{P_{iM}} \qquad i=1,2 \qquad (4m\text{-}5m)$$
$$\frac{\partial F_{iM}}{\partial L_{iM}} = \frac{w_{iM}}{P_{iM}} \qquad i=1,2 \qquad (6m\text{-}7m)$$

Full-employment condition:
$$K_{2P} = K_P$$
$$K_{1M} + K_{2M} = K_M \tag{8m}$$
$$L_{1M} + L_{2M} = L_M \tag{9m}$$
$$L_M + L_{2P} = L_G \tag{10m}$$

Minimum-wage condition in case of labour surplus:
$$w_{2M} = \delta_E(\lambda P_{2P} + (1-\lambda)P_{2M}) \tag{11m}$$

a) Before the „dual price system":
$$\lambda = \frac{Y_{2P}}{Y_{2P} + Y_{2M}}$$

b) During the „dual price system":
$$\lambda = \frac{Y_{2P}^P}{Y_{2P}^P + Y_{2P}^+ + Y_{2M}} = \frac{wY_{2P}}{Y_{2P} + Y_{2M}} \text{ with: } w = \frac{Y_{2P}^P}{Y_{2P}} \text{ and } 1-w = \frac{Y_{2P}^+}{Y_{2P}}$$

c) After „freeing up" of the price control: $(P_{2P} = P_{2M})$
$$w_{2M} = \delta_E P_{2M} \tag{11m-b}$$

Unifying of wage rate in a case without labour surplus:
$$w_{1M} = w_{2M} \tag{11m-c}$$

Wage relation between the two segments:
$$w_{2M} = v_E w_P \tag{12m}$$

Savings from the labour income:
$$S = s_{wM}(w_{1M}L_{1M} + w_{2M}L_{2M}) + s_{wP}w_{2P}L_P$$

Distribution of savings for investment:
a) Total saving for planned segment: $\kappa = 1$
b) Total saving for market segment: $\kappa = 0$
c) Distribution according to capital ratio: $\kappa = \dfrac{K_P}{K_P + K_M}$

Commodity demand:
$$NC_P^d = (1 - s_{wP})w_P L_P + (1 - s_r)r_P K_P, \tag{5p}$$
$$NC_M^d = (1 - s_{wM})(w_{1M}L_{1M} + w_{2M}L_{2M}) + (1 - s_r)r_M K_M \tag{13m}$$
$$NI_P^d = s_r r_P K_P + \kappa S \tag{6p}$$
$$NI_M^d = s_r r_M K_M + (1 - \kappa)S \tag{14m}$$
$$Y_{1M}^d = \varepsilon L_G. \tag{15m}$$

Disequilibrium of the planned segment:
$$E = NC_P^d - P_{2P}C_{2P} \qquad (6p)$$

Market-balance condition:
$$Y_{1M}^d = Y_{1M} \qquad (16m)$$
$$P_{2M}I_{2M} + P_{2P}I_{2P} = NI_M^d + NI_P^d \qquad (17m)$$
$$P_{2M}C_{2M} + P_{2P}C_{2P} + P_{1M}Y_{1M} = NC_M^d + NC_P^{'d} \qquad (18m)$$

Capital accumulation:
$$K_{2P}(t+1) = K_{2P}(t) + \frac{s_rP K_P(t) + \kappa S}{\overline{P_2}} - \delta K_{2P}(t) \qquad (A)$$
$$K_M(t+1) = K_M(t) + \frac{s_rM K_M(t) + (1-\kappa)S}{\overline{P_2}} - \delta K_M(t) \qquad (B)$$

Population growth:
$$L_G(t+1) = (1+\rho_L)L_G(t) \qquad (C)$$

Technological progress:
$$\gamma_i = \gamma_0 e^{\lambda_i t} \qquad i=1,2 \qquad (D\text{-}E)$$

6.2. Comparative Static with Numerical Simulations

6.2.1 The Basic Transition Path

With parameters and initial values chosen as in the following table, we may beging the numerical simulation. First, we compute the basic evolutionary path. The basic path is a growth path of the model with the most simple parameter combination, in which the planned segment is assumed not to make any adjustment to the market situation. It serves as a basis for comparison to demonstrate the impact of the variation of economic parameters and the influence of the different policies on the transition process.

Table 6.3 Parameters for the basic path

α_1=0.25	β_1=0.75	γ_1=0.7	α_2=0.6	β_2=0.4	γ_2=7
δ=0.05	υ_E=0.8	P_{2P}=1	w_P=630	δ_E=400	ε=0.75
s_{rP}=0.8	s_{wP}=0.05	s_{rM}=0.8	s_{wM}=0.05	κ=3	μ=2
ρ_L=0.027	λ_1=0	λ_2=0	Km=1000	Kp=6000	Lg=4

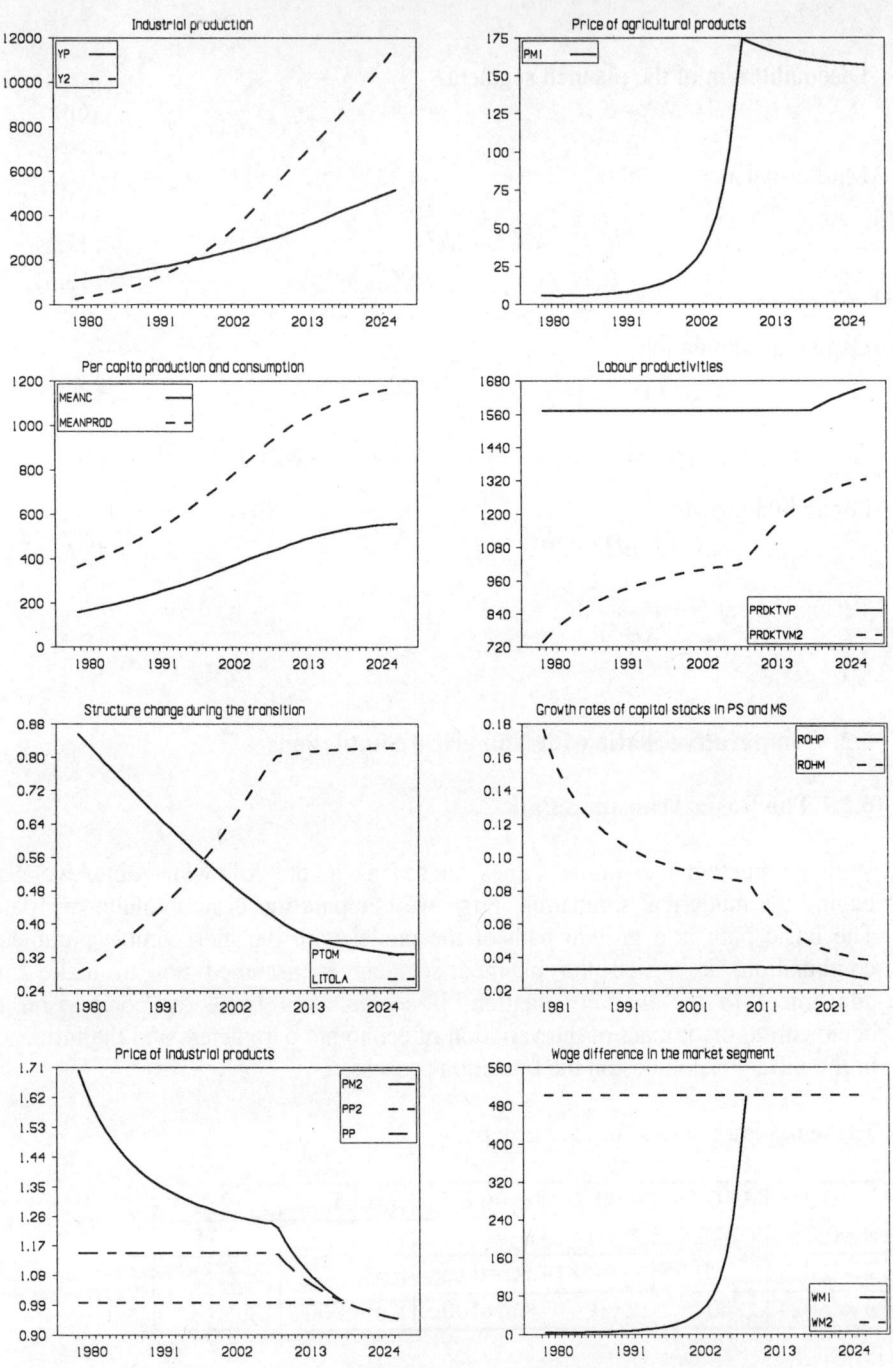

Graph 6.1 Transition path of the basic simulation

The evolution process of the system along the basic path is shown in **Graph 6.1**. It is easy to see that two processes are going on parallel - the industrialisation process and the transition process. In the third graph on the left hand side, the two curves show the decreasing share of the productive capital stock of the planned segment (PTOM) in the economy and the increasing share of labour force employed in the industrial sector (LITOLA), respectively. The first graph on the left hand side shows that during the transition process, production is growing in both segments (YP for planned segment, Y2 for market segment) and that production in the market segment will surpass that of the planned segment. Although the planned segment may also grow moderately during the transition process its share in the economy decreases continuously. The third graph on the right hand side shows the growth rate of capital stocks in the planned segment (ROHP) and in the market segment (ROHM), respectively. The main driving forces for the transition process are the advantages in the market segment — the higher prices and the lower wage rate. In the fourth graph on the left hand side, the three curves are the market price for industrial products (PM2), the planned price for industrial products (PP2) and the average price (PP), respectively. At the beginning of the transition, the production capacity in the market segment is relatively low in comparison to the demand, thus the market price reaches the highest level. The difference between the planned price and the market price decreases with the growth of the production capacity in the market segment. With labour surplus in the economy, the wage-price ratio(wage to average price) is fixed on a constant level, which is determined exogenously. This is expressed in the last graph on the right hand side of Graph 6.1.

The average price, therefore, does not change (we have chosen the wage rate as numéraire.), as long as labour surplus prevails. With the labour movement from agriculture into industry, the labour surplus situation diminishes. The minimum wage constraint becomes no longer binding, as soon as the wage in the agricultural sector reaches the level in the industrial sector. The last graph on the right hand side shows the approach of the wage rate in the agricultural sector to that in the industrial sector. The increase of the wage rate in agriculture (WM1) is supported by rising price of agricultural products. In the first graph on the right hand side, we see that the price of agricultural products (PM1) rises during the industrialisation process. It decreases when the labour surplus disappears. The time at which the labour surplus disappears is expressed in the last graph on the left hand side through the unification of the two wage rates (WM1 and WM2). In the last graph on the left hand side, it is shown through the turning point on the market price curve (PM2). After this point a labour surplus exits no longer. Consequently, the real wage raises after this point. This is expressed by the decreasing average price after the turning point. With the procession of transition, the market price falls to the level of the planned price, which is shown in the graph by the cross point, at which all three curves run together. After this point, the planned price is forced to follow the market price. Because the capital stock increases during the transition, both the per capita production (MEANPROD) and the per capita consumption (MEANC) increase (see the second graph on the left hand side). It is noteworthy that not every one profits from the increasing per capita consumption. Only farmers and capitalists gain more consumption from this increment. The industrial workers can not benefit from this increment because their real wage rate does not change as long as a labour surplus exits. They profit from the increase after the labour surplus is totally absorbed.

6.2.2 Influence of Population Growth

The influence of the population growth on the dynamic process is shown by a bundle of curves in **Graph 6.2**, each of which is given a number from 1 to 6 and corresponds to the growth of population at the rate of 0.027, 0.02, 0.015, 0.01, 0.005, and 0.0 per year, respectively. PTOM is the share of productive capital stock of the planned segment in the economy. LPTOM is the share of labour employment in the planned segment. With the disappearance of labour surplus, the real wage rises in the market segment. The employment in the market segment adjusts to this new real wage and decreases. However, after shifting to the new level, employment in the market segment still grows faster than in the planned segment. Hence, there are two turning points along each LPTOM curve. Obviously, the growth in population postpones the development. The transition process is also delayed in the sense that the stage of forced adjustment comes later.

6.2.3 Influence of Technical Progress on Transition

We will consider here only the neutral technical progress, which is expressed by the increase of the technical coefficient $\gamma_i = \gamma_0 e^{\lambda_i t}$ The curves from number 1 to number 6 in the **Graph 6.3**. correspond to $\lambda_i = 0.0, 0.005, 0.01, 0.015, 0.02$ and 0.025, respectively. Technical progress has a positive effect on the economy, both for the planned segment and the market segment. With technical progress, productivity and the per capita consumption both rise. In the case of labour surplus, technical progress at first favours the capital income because the real wage rate is repressed on a fixed level due to labour surplus. Owing to the wage advantage, capital income is more favoured through technical progress in the market segment than in the planned segment. Therefore, technical progress accelerates the growth in the market segment more than in the planned segment. Hence, it also accelerates the extrinsic transition. The impact of

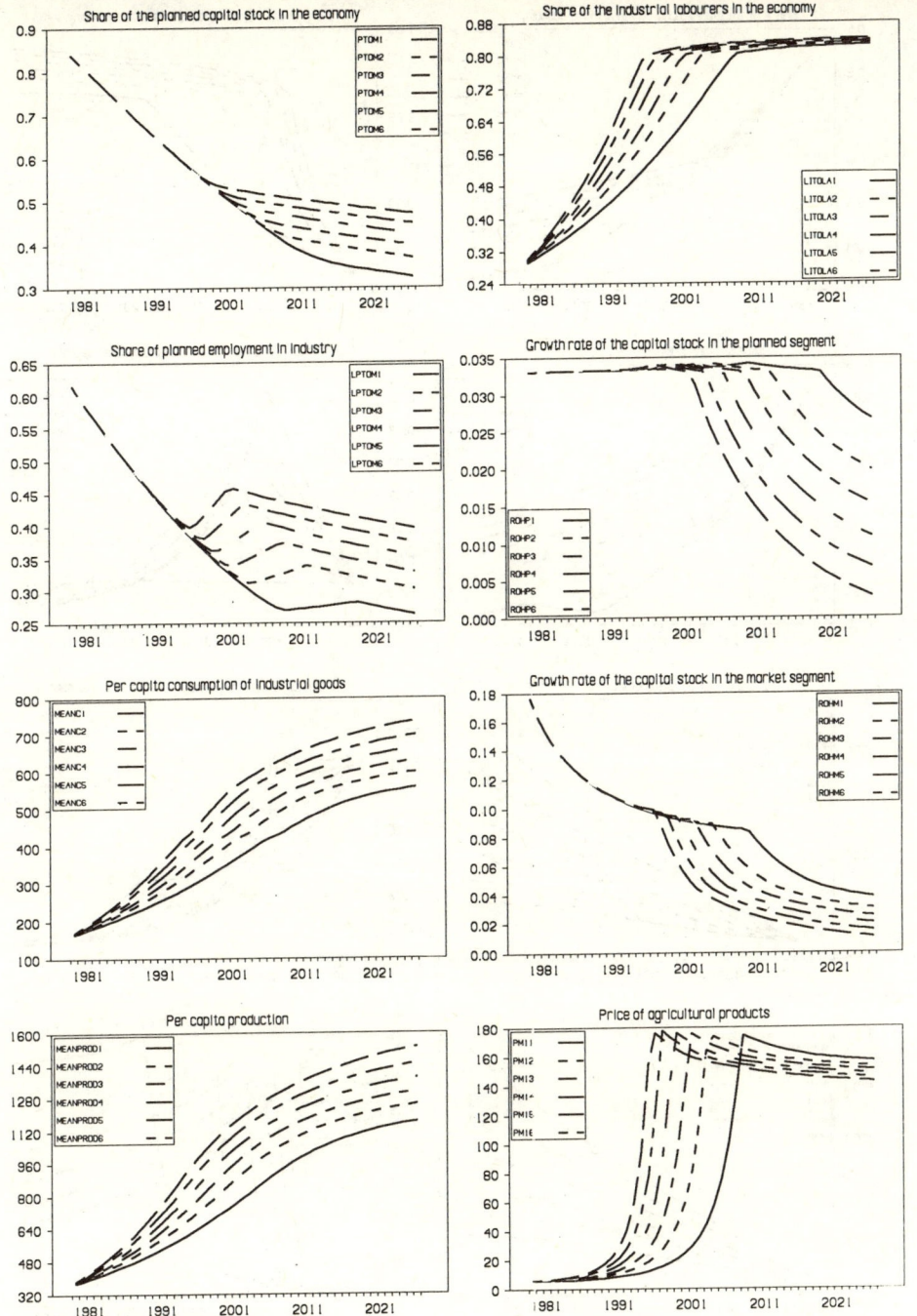

Graph 6.2 Influence of population growth on the transition path

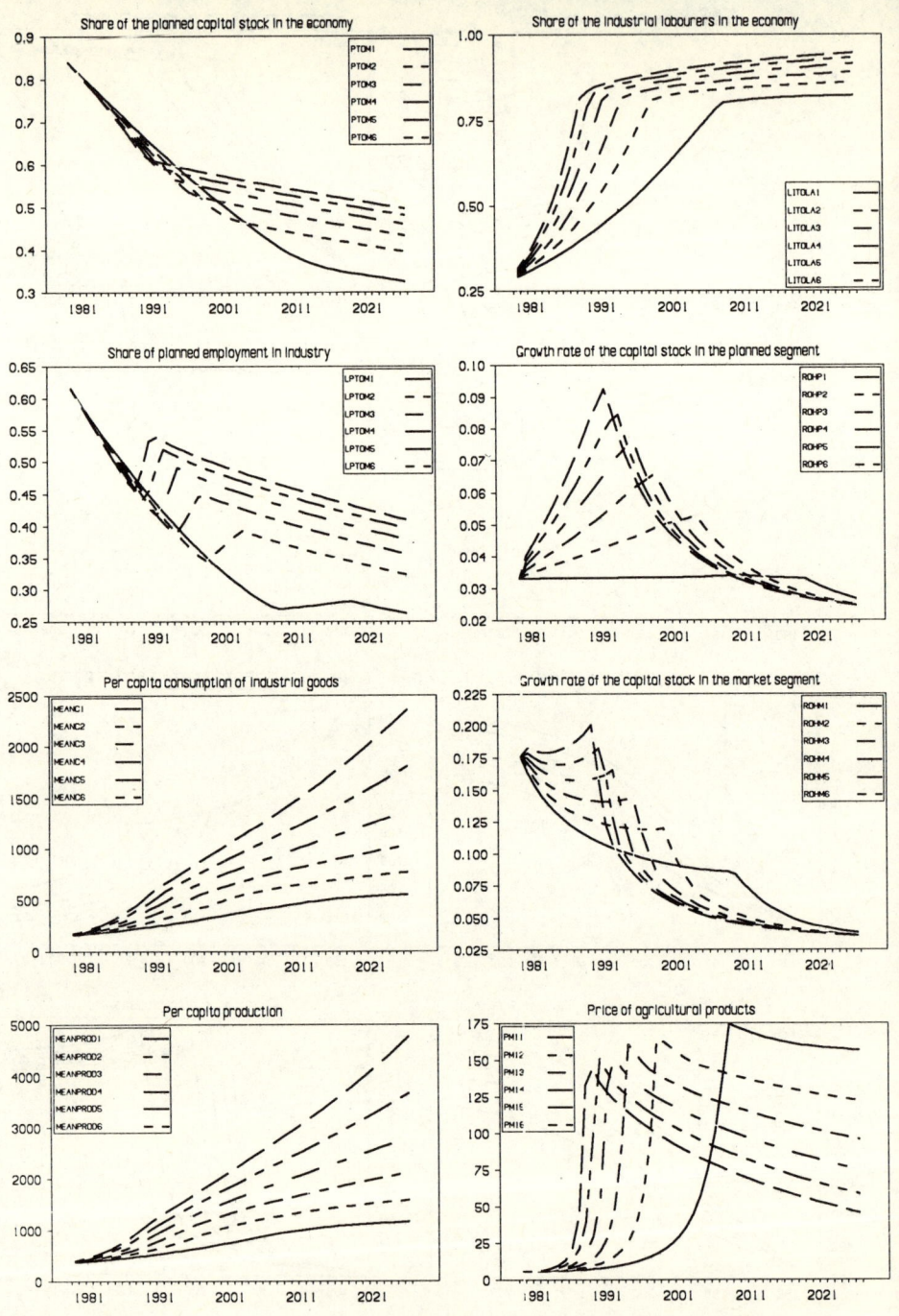

Graph 6.3 Influence of technical progress on the transition path

technical progress also has effects on the intrinsic transition. Through the shortening of the industrialisation process, labour surplus is absorbed earlier. Consequently, the forced adjustment takes place earlier. In this sense, technical progress accelerates the transition process. The industrial workers can not benefit directly from the technical progress at the beginning due to labour surplus. But they will profit from the technical progress in the future because technical progress will shorten the industrialisation process and the time point of a real wage increase comes earlier.

6.2.4 Savings and the Distribution

The impact of different distributions of savings for investment between the two segments is shown in **Graph 6.4**. fnz=1 means that savings from the labour income are invested only in the planned segment; fnz=2 is for the case of a constant distribution between the two segments; with fnz=3 we mean the case, in which the savings are distributed to the share of capital stock of each segment. The curves in **Graph 6.4** show the paths of transition simulated with the following combination of parameters.

1	$s_{rP}=0.8$	$s_{wP}=0.05$	$s_{rM}=0.8$	$s_{wM}=0.05$	fnz=3
2	$s_{rP}=0.8$	$s_{wP}=0.15$	$s_{rM}=0.8$	$s_{wM}=0.15$	fnz=3
3	$s_{rP}=0.8$	$s_{wP}=0.05$	$s_{rM}=0.8$	$s_{wM}=0.05$	fnz=2
4	$s_{rP}=0.8$	$s_{wP}=0.15$	$s_{rM}=0.8$	$s_{wM}=0.15$	fnz=2
5	$s_{rP}=0.8$	$s_{wP}=0.05$	$s_{rM}=0.8$	$s_{wM}=0.05$	fnz=1
6	$s_{rP}=0.8$	$s_{wP}=0.15$	$s_{rM}=0.8$	$s_{wM}=0.10$	fnz=1

As we have discussed in chapter 5, the distribution of savings between the two segments is essential to the shares of the two segments in the economy. Hence, for the extrinsic transition the reform of the financial market is of great importance. The first graph on the right hand side in **Graph 6.4.** shows clearly the influence of the financial market on the extrinsic transition. Although driven by the lower price in the market segment, the forced adjustment would not take place without the absorption of labour surplus. The planned segment, with a superior share in the economy, could resist such force and the forced adjustment may not take place. In this sense, the reform of the financial market is key to the transition process.

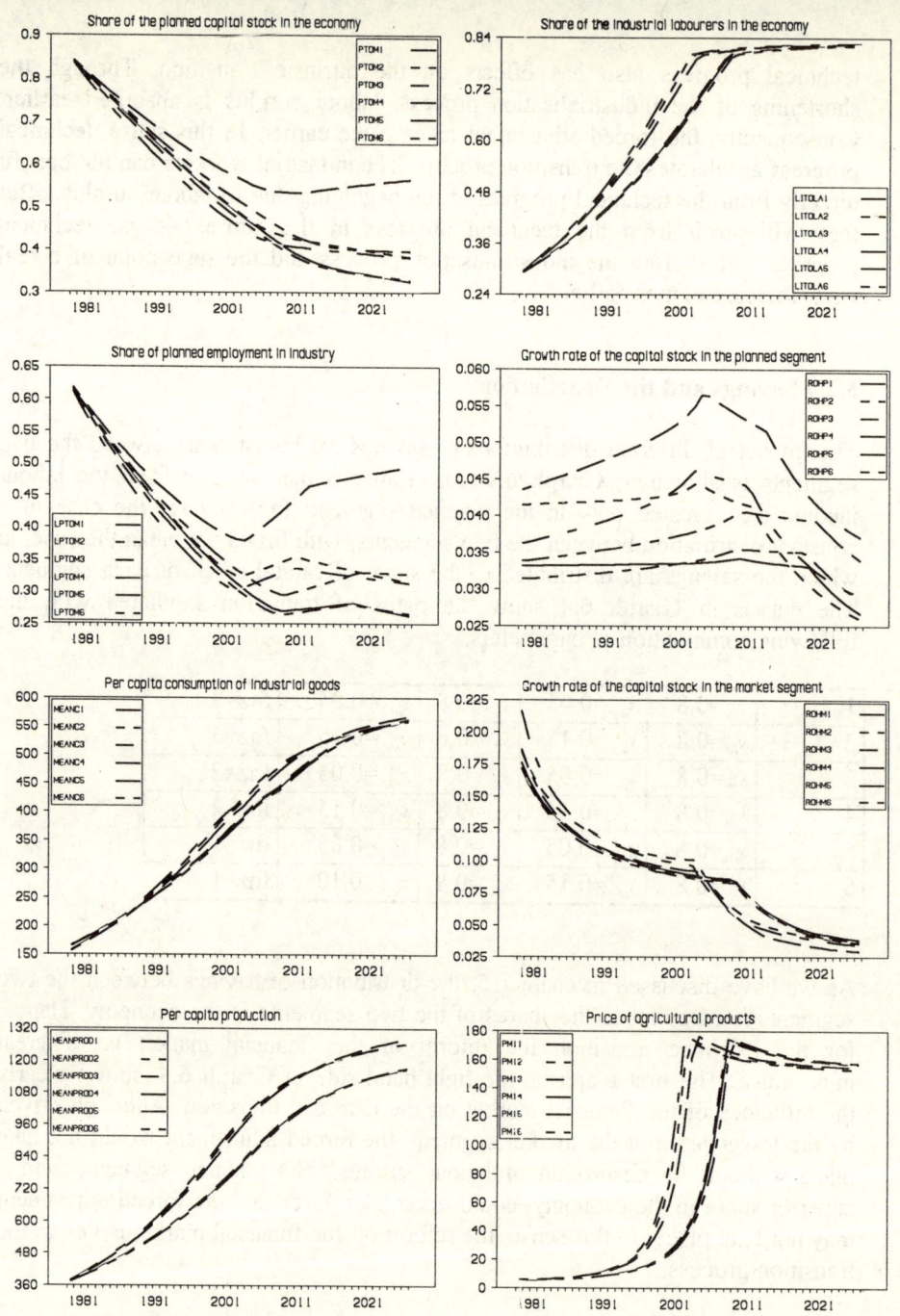

Graph 6.4 Influence of the finance market reform on the transition path

6.2.5 Adjustment in the Planned Segment

Graph 6.5 demonstrates the adjustment of the planned segment to the market situation. It is supposed that the adjustment begins with a dual price system. One way is to keep a constant share of the mandatory plan. An alternative is to reduce the share of the mandatory plan with time, until the price control is totally „freed up". The price reform is supposed to be introduced at 6-th period, and the share of the mandatory plan decreases with time linearly: $w = w_o \cdot (T-t)$. w is the share of planned quantities. T is the planned length of adjustment. In T periods the share of mandatory plan will be zero. Gragh 6.5 shows the influence of the length of the price reform on the transition process. The curves from number 1 to number 6 on **Graph 6.5** correspond to the following chosen parameters.

1	2	3	4	5	6
wo=0%	wo=5%	wo=7%	wo=9%	wo=11%	wo=15%
T=∞	T=20	T=15	T=11	T=9	T=6

The influence of the starting point of the price reform on the general transition process is shown on **Graph 6.6**. The starting points are chosen to be t = ∞, 15, 11, 7, 5, and 3, which correspond to the curves from number 1 to number 6.

The dual price system as an adjustment of the planned segment to the market situation makes the planned segment vital and gives it better chance to survive in the system. With the introduction of the dual price, the price in the planned segment rises and the capital income rises as well. Hence, the growth rate of the planned segment increases. This slows down the decreasing share of the planned segment in the economy. The increment of the growth rate in the planned segment reaches the maximum effect by totally giving up price control. The difference of growth between the two segments is then at the least. Choices of different starting points and lengths of the price reform have influence on the share of the planned segment in the economy during the transition process. The price reform has no significant impact on the industrialisation process. Nor has the price reform significant influence on the overall production and consumption. The stage of forced adjustment is almost independent from the starting point of the voluntary adjustment[87].

---

[87] The starting points of the price reform do not have significant influence on the equilibrium state in these simulations, because we have set the production capacity of the market segment at a rather high level.

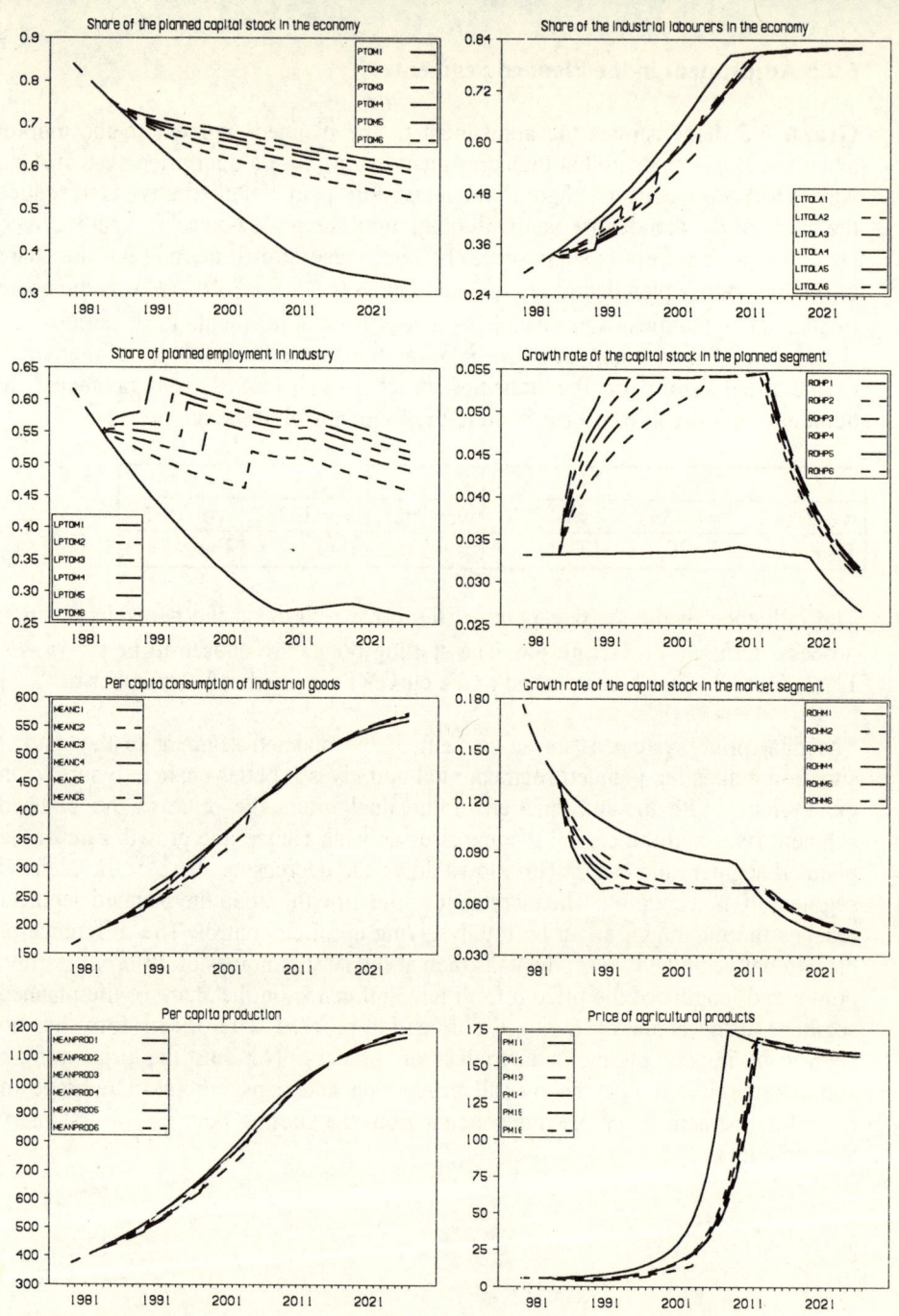

Graph 6.5 Influence of price reform on the transition path

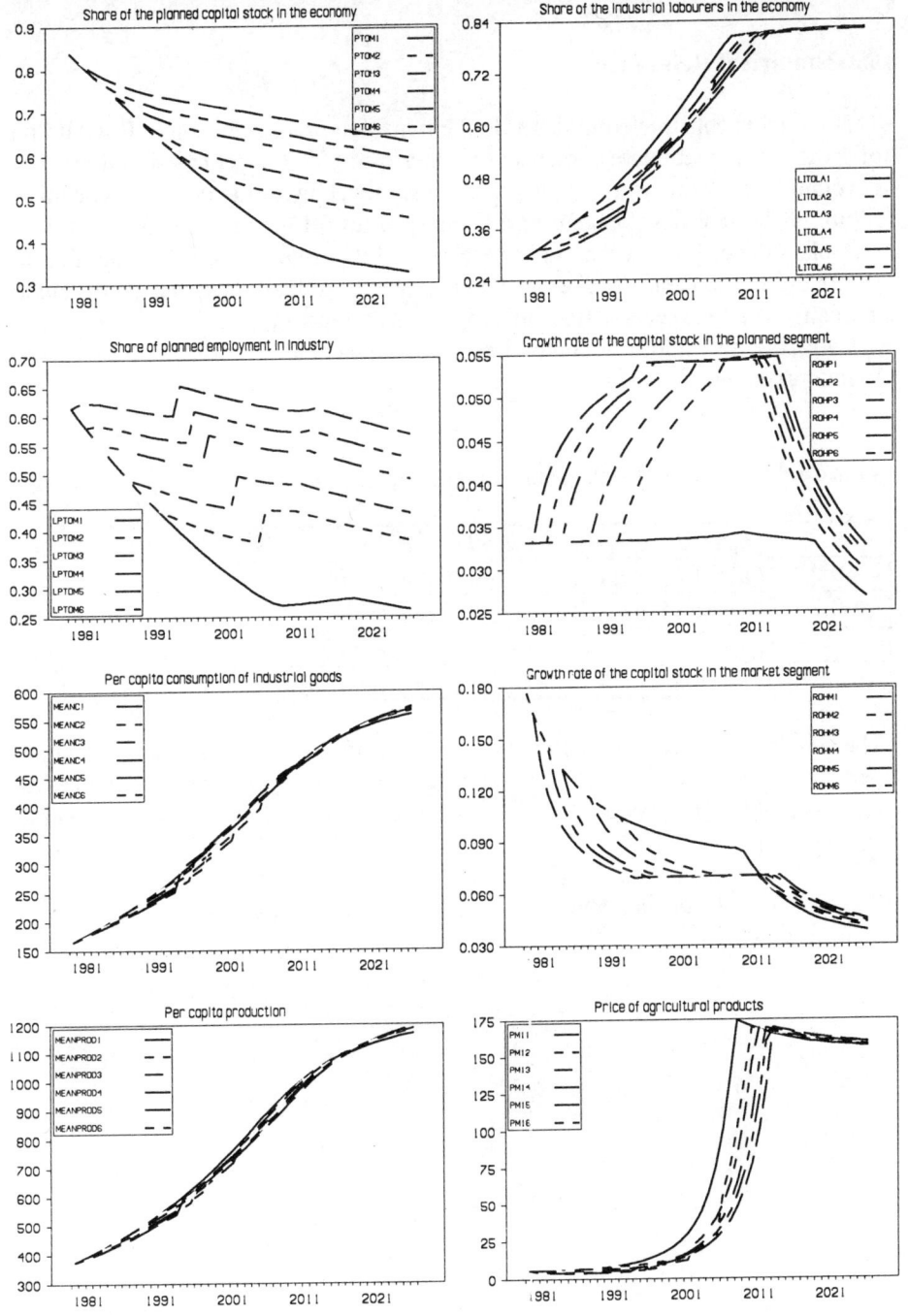

Graph 6.6 Influence of the staring of price reform on the transition path

6.3. Empirical Relevance

This model is constructed to describe the transition process in China. It would be of great theoretical interest to check whether or not the model can return the real development. Owing to the highly simplified modelling of the complex system, a fitting of the real development or an empirical test of the model would not be a suitable subject here. It may only be expected that the model should be able to give a correct tendency of the development if we model the policies as executed in reality. In this section, the numerical results and the real development are placed side by side for comparison. The numerical simulation is run with following parameters:

Table 6.4 Parameters for the simulation of realised development

$\alpha_1=0.25$	$\beta_1=0.75$	$\gamma_1=0.7$	$\alpha_2=0.6$	$\beta_2=0.4$	$\gamma_2=7$
$\delta=0.05$	$\upsilon_E=0.7$	$P_{2P}=1$	$w_P=630$	$\delta_E=400$	$\varepsilon=0.75$
$s_{rP}=0.75$	$s_{wP}=0.15$	$s_{rM}=0.8$	$s_{wM}=0.1$	fnz=3	$\mu=2$
	$\lambda_1=0$	$\lambda_2=0$	$T_{dual}=7$	wo=0.07	
Km=1000	Kp=6000				

The simulation is made from 1978 to 1992. The price reform began at the seventh period ($T_{dual}=7$) in the simulation because the dual price system was introduced in reality in 1984. For the total labour force L_G we have used the real data instead to simulate it.

Some results of the simulation are given through following tables and graphs for comparison.

Table 6.5 Industrial Production(simulated)

Year	Yp	Ym2	Share of Yp	Share of Ym2
1978	1173,19	319,29	0,79	0,21
1979	1193,16	374,66	0,76	0,24
1980	1213,49	434,88	0,74	0,26
1981	1234,20	500,42	0,71	0,29
1982	1255,28	571,77	0,69	0,31
1983	1276,75	649,45	0,66	0,34
1984	1298,62	718,58	0,64	0,36
1985	1325,42	791,76	0,63	0,37
1986	1356,22	869,52	0,61	0,39
1987	1390,52	952,39	0,59	0,41
1988	1428,05	1040,85	0,58	0,42
1989	1468,69	1135,34	0,56	0,44
1990	1512,37	1236,45	0,55	0,45
1991	1559,12	1344,70	0,54	0,46
1992	1608,97	1460,54	0,52	0,48
1993	1662,02	1584,56	0,51	0,49
1994	1718,36	1717,51	0,50	0,50
1995	1778,14	1859,89	0,49	0,51
1996	1841,50	2012,41	0,48	0,52

Y2 is the industrial production in the market segment. Yp is the industrial production in the planned segment.

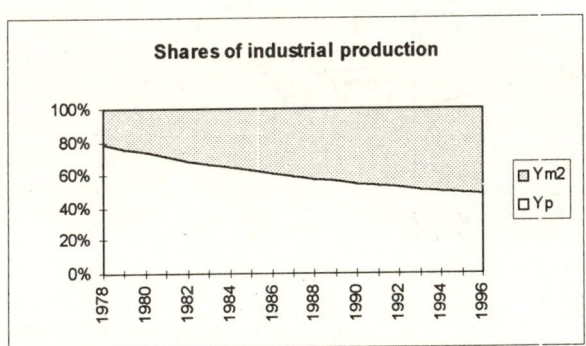

Graph 6.7 Composition of industrial production(simulated)

Table 6.6 Realised industrial gross output value (in 100 Mio. yuan)

Year	Production of non-state-owned enterprises	Production of state-owned enterprises	Share of non state-owned production	Share of state-owned production
1978	948	3289	0,22	0,78
1979	1008	3673	0,22	0,78
1980	1214,51	3915	0,24	0,76
1981	1294,6	4073	0,24	0,76
1982	1445,6	4326	0,25	0,75
1983	1671,6	4739	0,26	0,74
1984	2278,6	5262	0,30	0,70
1985	3296,59	6302	0,34	0,66
1986	4059,94	6971	0,37	0,63
1987	5283,23	8250	0,39	0,61
1988	7413,68	10351	0,42	0,58
1989	8916,56	12342	0,42	0,58
1990	9813,44	13063	0,43	0,57
1991	11694,42	14954	0,44	0,56
1992	16607,42	17824	0,48	0,52
1993	24615	22724	0,52	0,48
1994	40287	26200	0,60	0,40

Source: Chinese Statistic Year book 1993 p.412; 1995 p.375

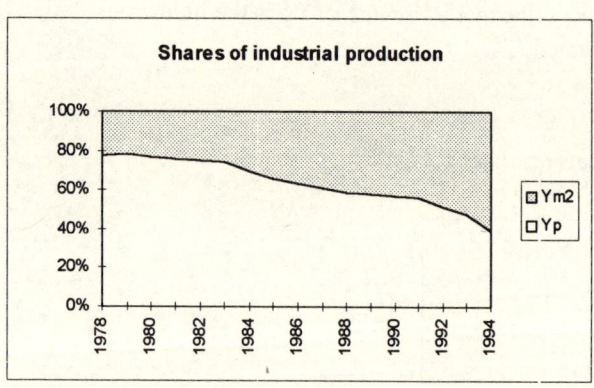

Graph 6.8 Composition of industrial production(realised)

Table 6.7 Simulated abour distribution (in 100 mio.)

Year	Lp	Lm2	Lm1	Lg
1978	0,74	0,45	2,82	4,02
1979	0,76	0,51	2,84	4,10
1980	0,77	0,57	2,90	4,24
1981	0,78	0,63	2,96	4,37
1982	0,80	0,70	3,03	4,53
1983	0,81	0,78	3,06	4,64
1984	0,82	0,81	3,18	4,82
1985	0,84	0,86	3,29	4,99
1986	0,86	0,92	3,35	5,13
1987	0,88	0,98	3,42	5,28
1988	0,91	1,05	3,48	5,43
1989	0,93	1,13	3,47	5,53
1990	0,96	1,21	3,50	5,67
1991	0,99	1,30	3,54	5,84
1992	1,02	1,40	3,52	5,94
1993	1,06	1,51	3,46	6,02
1994	1,09	1,62	3,43	6,15
1995	1,13	1,75	3,37	6,25
1996	1,17	1,88	3,31	6,36

Lp is the labour force employed in the planned segment, L1 is the labour force in agriculture, L2 is labour force employed in the industrial sector in the market segment. LG is the total labour force.

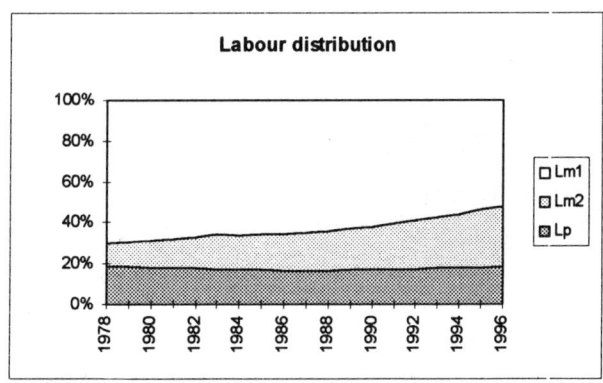

Graph 6.9 Labour distribution (simulated)

Table 6.8 Realised labour distribution (in 10 thausend)

Year	Labour in state-owned enterprises	Labour in non state-owned enterprises	Labour in agricultural sector	Total labour
1978	7451	4889	27812	40152
1979	7693	5215	28116	41024
1980	8019	5505	28837	42361
1981	8372	5650	29703	43725
1982	8630	5910	30755	45295
1983	8771	6202	31463	46436
1984	8637	8800	30760	48197
1985	8990	10797	30086	49873
1986	9333	11896	30053	51282
1987	9654	12934	30195	52783
1988	9984	13828	30522	54334
1989	10108	13648	31573	55329
1990	10346	13648	32746	56740
1991	10664	14212	33484	58360
1992	10889	15322	33177	59432
1993	10920	17385	31911	60220
1994	11214	17619	32637	61470

Source: Chinese Statistic Year Book 1993 p. 97 p.395; 1995 p.85

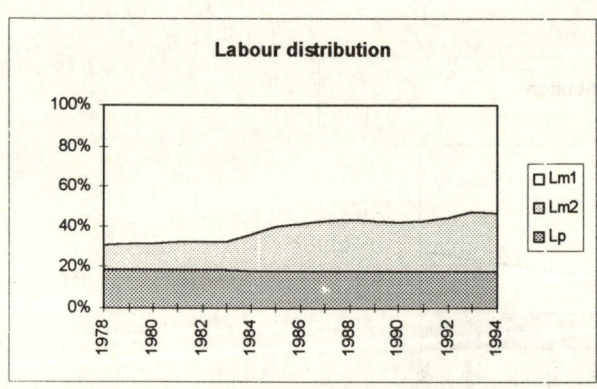

Graph 6.10 Labour distribution (realised)

During the economic reform in the last 15 years, the non-planned economy has experienced a flourishing development and is becoming more and more important in the whole economy. According to official statistics, the industrial production value of the non-state-owned economy has surpassed that of the planned economy in 1992. Because the gross production is valued at current price and hence strongly influenced by inflation, a direct comparison with the absolute value will make little sense. It is interesting to see that the numerical simulation can describe the changing share in the industrial production very well.

In this model, we have explained the phenomena of changing share through the advantage of prices, the advantage of the wage rate and the flexible structure of production. We can now verify these through empirical statistics.

Table 6.9 Difference of average wage between the state-owned enterprises and non state-owned enterprises (Yuan/year)

Year	Average wage in non-state-owned enterprises	Average in state-owned enterprises	Wage ratio
1978	380.45	628.10	1.65
1979	421.94	687.64	1.63
1980	477.83	781.89	1.64
1981	511.50	788.34	1.54
1982	551.61	820.39	1.49
1983	582.16	852.81	1.46
1984	650.91	1013.08	1.56
1985	752.70	1183.54	1.57
1986	820.10	1380.05	1.68
1987	945.06	1511.29	1.60
1988	1120.31	1809.90	1.62
1989	1237.64	2028.10	1.64
1990	1322.42	2246.28	1.70
1991	1455.71	2433.42	1.67
1992	1712.00	2837.73	1.66

Source: Chinese Statistic Year Book p.397 p.395 p.121 and p.37

From **Table 6.9** we can see that the ratio of the average wage is almost constant around 1,6. The fact that the average wage in the non-state-owned sector is always smaller that in the state-owned sector is due to the existence of surplus supply of labour in the economy.

Table 6.10 Price ratio between market price and planned price (simulated and realised)

Year	Simulated price ratio	Real price ratio
1978	1.79	1.69
1979	1.71	1.57
1980	1.64	1.48
1981	1.58	1.49
1982	1.54	1.48
1983	1.50	1.48
1984	1.38	1.43
1985	1.30	1.28
1986	1.24	1.17
1987	1.19	1.17
1988	1.16	1.17
1989	1.13	1.12
1990	1.10	1.07
1991	1.08	1.05
1992	1.06	1.03
1993	1.05	
1994	1.03	

Source: Chinese Statistic Year Book 1993 p.256

The price difference between the list price and free market price is shown in **Table 6.10**. It is noteworthy that the price difference between the planned and the market segment was decreasing with time. In the model we have explained this kind of relation through the growing capacity of the production and thus the supply from the market segment.

Through the comparison of the simulated data and the realised data, we can conclude that this simple model is able to explain the real development during the economic reform properly. Especially the special features of the development in the Chinese economy during the reform - the fast growth of the market segment, the industrialisation process, and the labour movement are described by the simulation quite well. The price development can also be described in the model. One Short-coming in the model is that the wage difference is set only exogenously and is not endogenously explained. However, the model provides a theoretical understanding of the complex economic phenomena of the transition process through a clearly defined structure.

Concluding Remarks

Complicated economic phenomena during the transition from plan to market can be classified in intrinsic and extrinsic transition, according to the cause of the transitional phenomena. The global behaviour of an economy in the transition process depends on which kind of transition plays the dominant role during the transition process. While the intrinsic transition, touched off by some reform polices, is always accompanied by „shocks" and, thus produces disturbances in the economy, the extrinsic transition, driven by the growth of the market activities, is a smoother process. The approach of this classification makes it possible to model the complex transition process with conventional methods of neo-classic theory. The extrinsic transition can be well captured in the framework of a growth theory. The intrinsic transition can be modelled as the impact of the political instrument on the planned economic activities and thus the whole economy. This two-fold modelling of the transition process only works well if the extrinsic transition plays the governing role in the transition process.

The transition from plan to market in China, characterised by „growing out of plan", is typically dominated by the extrinsic transition in which growth, especially the faster growth of the market segment, is the most important driving force of the transition. This particular „Chinese way of transition" is marked by a decentralised industrialisation process during the reform era.

Before the economic reform, Chinese industrialisation followed the Soviet-type way. In this mode of industrialisation, the central planning controlled the whole economic activities. Because agriculture should provide the „surplus" for industrialisation, the price of agricultural products was kept at a very low level. Since consumption should give way to the „productive accumulation", the wage rate in industry was also set at very low level. (The planning authority was able to control the income of farmers by controlling the price because the price for agricultural products determined the income of farmers.) Consequently, although the economy had grown at a rather high rate, the living standard had hardly improved. The economic reform, led by the rural reform, has significantly changed the mechanism of industrialisation. It „freed" the economic force from the bureaucratic administration. The improved income on rural areas, the existing technological conditions, the liberalised economic environment, and the established incentive stimulated and enforced a decentralised industrialisation process. A market-economic segment emerged during this process. The market segment took advantage of the existing planned segment and could develop faster than the planned segment. This formed the particular Chinese way of transition.

The faster growth of the market segment can be traced back to three economic reasons rooted in existing Chinese economic conditions and in its history. 1. The huge reservoir of the labour force in China, i.e. the existing labour surplus, made it possible to use labour at a lower wage rate in the market segment than in the planned segment. Taking advantage of the lower price in planned segment, the market segment can even work with a marginal labour productivity lower than the minimum consumption level. This advantage in labour usage prevails, as long as the industrialisation process continues and a significant wage difference between the rural and urban areas exists. In this context, the industrialisation process plays a key role during the transition from plan to market. 2. Owing to the price mechanism of the market, producers in the market segment can always sell their products at a higher (or not lower to be precise) price level than that in the planned segment, in which the price was set by the planning authority. The price difference was legitimated by the reform policy of the „two tiers"-system that was historically founded by Chinese economic development. The different wages and the different prices lead to the result that the capital income in the marker segment is much higher than that in the planned segment. This in turn leads to a faster growth in production capacity in the market than in the planned segment. However, the price advantage disappears as soon as the price reform in the planned segment is completed. The wage advantage exists until the industrialisation process is finished. 3. The flexible allocation of the market is another reason why the market segment can grow faster. The investors of the market segment can choose activities selectively in the most profitable branches, while the planned segment has to provide some products and services which are not profitable, and no investors of the market segment are hence willing to produce. At this point, we touch the field of market failure and public economy, whose dimensions reach far beyond the scope of this thesis. However, in this context we know that the value of the planned segment can not only be judged by its growth.

The intrinsic transition in China can be viewed as the adjustment process of the planned segment to the continuously changing economic situation, driven by the market force. The price reform could reduce the price disadvantage of the planned segment against the market segment and accelerate its growth. The reform on the labour market would reduce the disadvantage in labour usage in the long run. However, with these reform policies the planned segment loses its planned economic nature. The disadvantages can only be totally removed if the planned segment can perform identically to the market segment, which implies that the planned segment itself would become a market segment.

We have concluded that the reform of the financial market is key to the transition process. If the financial market is still administratively controlled and a „favour-planned-segment" policy is pursued, the transition process will be ended at a certain constant mixture, with planned segment on the one side and the market segment on the other. The planned economic activities may dominate in this situation. If the financial market is run somehow competitively, then the market segment will dominate in the long run. The price reform and the reform of the labour market can make the planned segment more market-like and hence enforce the intrinsic transition. However, timing of the reform policy may be crucial for the policy to have intended effect. The weight of the market segment in the economy is decisive whether a reform polcy may promote or impede the transition process. Reform measures remain active political choices of the policy-makers during the stage of voluntary adjustment. As soon as the industrialisation process is completed and the labour surplus disappears, reform measures are not political choices any longer. The planned segment then has to behave like the market segment in order to survive in the economy.

The impact of the transition on common welfare expressed by consumption is in general positive owing to the over all growth process. However, the average gain in welfare should be viewed differentially. The owners of the capital stocks profit the most from the transition process through high capital income. The farmer-workers who moved from agriculture into industry obtain more real income owing to the higher wage rate in the industrial sector. Farmers gain more income through the rising wage due to the rising prices of agriculture products. Workers in the state-owned enterprises could not benefit from the transition process. By contrast, they would suffer from the loss of real income due to rising prices. In this sense, the transition has a negative redistribution effect for the workers of the state-owned enterprises. But, this loss could be compensated if the planned wage rate would be set to guarantee a constant level of real income. However, this guarantee is made at the cost of the capital income in the planned segment, which weakens the growth of the planned segment. Hence, this guarantee can only be founded by a technical progress in the long run.

The transition process therefore promises a „golden future", only if the technical progress enforced by the transition can outweigh the negative redistribution effect of the transition.

References

Bornstein, Morris. (1974) „Comparative Economic Systems: Model and Cases", Richard D.Irwin, Inc. 1974, Homewood, London, Ontario.

Blank, Grant and Parish, William L. (1990), „Rural Industry and Nonfarm Employment: Comparative Perspectives", in Kwok R.Yin-Wang (1990), P.109-130.

Brown, Alan A. and Neuberger, Egon. (1974), „Basic Features of a Centrally Planned Economy" in Bornstein, Morris (1974) P.236.

Byrd, William A. (1987). „The two-tier plan/market system", Journal of Comparative Economics, 1987, Vol. 11, P.299

Byrd, William. A. (1991) „The Market Mechanism and Economic Reforms in China, M.E.Sharpe, Inc. 1991, Armonk, New York, London, P.19

Charemza, Wojciech. (1989), See: Davis, Christopher and Charemza, Wojciech (1989)

Cheetham, Russell J. (1972), See: Kelley, Allen C. (1972)

Chen, Pu (1990), „Charakterisirung der wirtschaflichen Gegebenheiten in der Volksrepublik China und der Versuch einer ökonomisch-theoretischen Analyse", Diplom-Thesis, University Bielefeld, Germany.

Cheng, Xuan (1990), „Problems of urbanization", in Kwok R.Yin-Wang (1990), P.65-77.

Conlisk, J. „Non-constant return to scale in a neoclassical growth model", International Economic Review Vol. 9, October 1968, P.369-73.

Davis, Christopher and Charemza, Wojciech (1989), „Models of Disequilibrium and Shortage in Centrally Planned Economics", Chapman and Hall, London, New York, 1989.

Ericson, R. „The second economy and resource allocation under central planning", Journal of Comparative Economics. 1984 Vol. 8. P.1-24.

Fan, Gang. (1994), „Dual-track transition in China", Economic Policy, December 1994, P.99

Hare, Paul. (1989) „The economics of shortage in centrally planned economies" in Davis and Charmeza (1989) P.49

Grosfeld, Irena. (1987), „Modelling planner behaviour: Poland 1956-1981", Journal of Comparative Economics 1987, Vol. 11, P.180-191.

Gruchy, Allen G. (1985) „Comparative Economic Systems: Competing Ways to Stability, Growth, and Welfare" 2nd Edition Translated by Xu Jiewen, Wang Lianshen and Liuzezen, Beijing.

Jefferson Gary H. and Xu, Wenyi (1991)," The impact of reform on socialist enterprises in transition: structure, conduct, and performance in Chinese industry", Journal of Comparative Economics, Vol. 15, 1991, P.45-64.

Jefferson, Gary H. and Rawski, G. Thomas.(1994). „Enterprises reform in Chinese industry", Journal of Economic Perspectives Spring 1994, Vol. 8 P.50

Kalecki (1972) „Theorie des Wachstums und der Planung in der sozailistischen Volkswirtschaft", Nomos Verlaggesellschaft, Baden-Baden.

Kelley, Allen C. Williamson, Jeffrey G. and Cheetham, Russell J. (1972), „Dualistic Economic Development", The University of Chicago Press, Chicago and London, 1972.

Kornai, J. (1980), „Economics of Shortage", Vol. 1, North-Holland, Amsterdam, 1980.

Krug, Barbara. (1986), „Preisreform in der VR China", Bericht des Bundesinstituts für ostwissenschaftliche und internationale Studien 1986 P.12

Kwok R.Yin-Wang (1990), Chinese Urban Reform: What Model Now? Share 1990, Armon, New York, London

Liu Zuofu and Wang Zhenzhi. (1986), „Socialist Price Theory", Chinese Publishing House of Finance and Economics, Beijing, 1986.

Marglin, Stephen A. (1984), „Growth, Distribution and Prices", Harvard University Press, Cambridge, Massachusetts, and London, 1984

Motoshige Itoh and Takashi Negishi (1987), „Disequilibrium Trade Theories", Harwood Academic Publishers GmbH Chur, Switerland, 1987.

Murrell, Peter. (1991), „Can neoclassical economics underpin the reform of centrally planned economy?", Journal of Economic Perspectives, Vol. 5, Fall 1991, P.59-76.

Naughton, Barry. (1990) „China's experience with guidance planning", Journal of Comparative Economics 1990 Vol. 14, P.743-67.

Panagariya, Arvind. (1990) „The parallel market in centrally planned economies: a dynamic analysis", Journal of Comparative Economics 1990 Vol. 14, P.353-371.

Parish, William L. (1990), „What Model Now?", in Kwok R.Yin-Wang (1990), P.3-17.

Perkins, Dwight H. (1990), „The Influence of Economic Reforms on China's Urbanization" in Kwok R.Yin-Wang (1990), P.78-106

Perkins, Dwight H. (1994), „Completing Chinese reform", Journal of Economic Perspectives", Spring 1994, P.22-46

Portes, Rechard. (1989), „The theory and measurement of macroeconomics disequilibrium in centrally planned economies", in Davis and Charemza (1989) P. 27.

Quandt, Richard E. (1989), „Disequilibrium econometrics for centrally planned economies" in Davis and Charemza (1989), P.181-204.

Rawski, G. Thomas. See Jefferson

Schmieding, Holger. (1993), „From plan to market: on the nature of transition crisis", Weltwirtschaftliches Archiv Vol.129(2) 1993; P. 216-253.
Sen, Amartya (1988): in Hand Book of Development Economics vol. 1, P.12 ff.

Shen, Guanbao. (1991), „Rural enterprises and urbanization", in „Chinese Urban Reform: What Model Now" by R.Yin-Wang Kwok et al, P.158

Takashi Negishi (1987),See: Motoshige Itoh and Takashi Negishi (1987)

Varian, Hal R. „Mikroökonomie", R.Oldenbourg Verlag München Wien, 1981.

Williamson, Jeffrey G. (1972), See Kelley, Allen C. (1972).

Wing Thye Woo (1994): „The art of reforming centrally planned economies: comparing China, Poland, and Russia, Journal of Comparative Economics. Vol. 18; P. 286.

Wu, Jinglian and Zhao, Renwei. (1987) „The dual pricing system in China's industry", Journal of Comparative Economics. 1987 Vol. 11, P.309-318

Zhao, Renwei. (1987), See Wu, Jinglian and Zhao, Renwei (1987).

Zhou, Huizhong. (1992), „An explanation of coexistence of taut planning and hidden reserves in centrally planned economies", Journal of Comparative Economics Vol. 16, 1992, P.456-78.

Zhou, Huizhong. (1993)," Plan-influencing and market fine-tuning", Journal of Economic Perspectives, Vol. 17, Sept. 1993, P.561-580.

Zhu, Xingcheng. (1984), „Financial Management in Industrial Enterprises", Publishing House of CCTV-University, Beijing, 1984.

Chinese Statistic Year Book 1988 Chinese Bureau of Statistics China, Statistics Publishing House, 1988, Beijing.

Chinese Statistic Year Book 1994 Chinese Bureau of Statistics China, Statistics Publishing House, 1994, Beijing.

Chinese Statistic Year Book 1995 Chinese Bureau of Statistics China, Statistics Publishing House, 1995, Beijing.

Peking Rundschau 1978, Vol. 52 P.13

Peking Rundschau 1980, Vol. 50 P.4

Peking Rundschau 1983, Vol. 50 P.22-26.

Caimao Jinji 1992, 3-15